Specialty advertising
in marketing

Specialty advertising in marketing

GEORGE L. HERPEL

and

RICHARD A. COLLINS

1972
DOW JONES-IRWIN, INC.
HOMEWOOD, ILLINOIS   60430

First Printing, January 1972
Second Printing, September 1972

Library of Congress Catalog Card No. 78–165355
Printed in the United States of America

Preface

CERTAINLY among the most difficult decisions in marketing are those having to do with promotional mix selection and subsequent evaluation. The possible alternatives are almost unlimited. Along with the many dynamic forces in the market place which can affect the success of any promotional strategy, the problems of coordination, of reacting to competition, and of dealing with the legal or social aspects of promotion, plus the efforts to maximize the effectiveness of the people involved, make this a vastly complex responsibility. Much assistance, research, and literature can be found regarding certain aspects of promotion. Other aspects have limited coverage, and a few (like specialty advertising) have had virtually no coverage at all. Since decisions are based on background information and facts, it is not surprising that perceptions of the role of this type of promotion and the decisions connected with it are subjective and quite nebulous.

The aim of the authors has been to bring together and relate the scattered reports and references in order to encourage more objectivity and provide a base for further study and research. A major limitation in the preparation of this book has been the scarcity of previous publications and data. With subsequent research and analysis trends will become more evident. Information vacuums do not make for objective acceptance in any field. This is particularly true of such a large and visual activity as promotion.

Very little has been written on specialty advertising nor is there anything taught in the colleges and universities at the present time. The authors have visualized this work as a reference source for the industry, but certain sections should be particularly appropriate for students who desire an insight into this specialized and effective field.

People presently in the industry or in positions of advertising and promotional counseling should have a broader understanding in order to perform their responsibilities most effectively. To bring the best professional service to clients, advertising agency personnel should have a full realization of and acquaintance with all means of reaching their clients' prospects and buyers. Consequently, certain parts of this book are intended to add to the knowledge of professional advertising management.

For those actively engaged in the industry, a limited number of the topics covered actually relate to "how to" increase performance. On top of this, anyone that expects continued success in specialty advertising should be sensitive to its history and development and should have not only a knowledge of its overall structure and an understanding of its problems, but also an awareness of the trends and opportunities which are likely to lie ahead. The authors feel that any "how to" approach is enhanced if questions are first covered that pertain to "how did we get here" and "where are we going." Experience and practicality are not totally isolated from the theories and research pertaining to the background of a broad field of activity.

The "Introduction" is included to get all readers to feel more involved in the field. The authors tried this simple experimental approach with several groups of students who had no previous concept of "specialty advertising" and who may even have doubted its existence. The groups were rather surprised at what they learned.

The first chapter is a general discussion of the concept and role of specialty advertising, and of some commonly used terms, typical products, and trade practices and problems, which sets the stage for more detailed discussion in later chapters. Chapter 2 concerns the history of specialty advertising. Since no one time period is isolated and unrelated, this chapter provides additional perspective and comprehension so the reader may understand the present situation and expected future developments.

Chapter 3 covers the place of specialty advertising in the marketing and promotional mix. Special reference is made to trends and basic needs in regard to evaluating combinations of factors in the promotional mix. The current methods of allocating funds to specialty advertising were investigated in a limited way by contacting a hundred users of specialty merchandise; the results of this investigation are presented. Another dimension of this research indicated how some companies feel this type of effort fits into their selling programs.

The general application of specialty advertising merchandising is covered in Chapter 4. Its challenges, limitations, and inability to overcome some older problems are discussed. Part of the chapter covers "how to" in the important areas of sales management and the sales process per se. How other practitioners in advertising, promotion, and sales view specialty advertising is, of course, vital to future progress and the directions the industry takes. These may well be some of the most fruitful areas of future study that the industry's association can undertake.

The fifth chapter is an examination of major behavorial aspects in marketing strategy to which specialty advertising relates. These are felt to be of particular importance in evaluating present acceptance of the industry. Also, it is essential to realize that major changes in behavior norms or value systems can affect future trends within the industry.

Chapter 6 capsulizes representative examples of marketing problems in which specialty advertising has been used, with comments for practitioners on "how to" relate these to major marketing problems. This is tied closely to the major environmental factors surrounding the industry, as covered in Chapter 7.

The final chapter is a broad overview of what's expected in the future. There is risk in attempting to forecast industry development since there are so many variables, many of which are uncontrollable. Yet some trends are apparent. In this regard, research was conducted with numerous members of the Specialty Advertising Association International. Special emphasis was devoted to a group organized as YESAA (Young Executives, Specialty Advertising Association). These members were quite cooperative, analytical, and vocal about what lies ahead. Without drawing any conclusions at this point, it was apparent that the younger men are sensitive to the "marketing concept," more acquainted with tools and techniques of progressive decision making, and less prone to be bound by traditions and practices of the past. The influences of the marketplace, customers, and competitive forces are all apparent to this group. And certainly, any future that can be developed is in their hands.

Because of the limitations encountered due to the scarcity of information and the restricted primary research, Appendix A lists prospective research projects that might be undertaken. It is hoped that much greater insight will be gained as new data are developed through such future research projects—not only projects that might be covered by Association efforts or related advertising groups, but also those offering some challenges which might be especially appropriate for academic research studies.

The authors wish to express appreciation to Robert Rollings, president of Specialty Advertising Association International (SAAI), and to his staff for their cooperation in developing concepts, carrying out research, and contributing ideas for expanded material. Unless otherwise indicated, all illustrations are through the courtesy of the Association. The elected officers of SAAI were most helpful and objective in their comments regarding the manuscript as it was developed. Marvin Spike, publisher of *The Counselor,* was especially cooperative in making file material and historical information available. Finally, the authors express appreciation to colleagues who generously contributed comments to the book while it was in the process of being completed.

December, 1971   GEORGE L. HERPEL
                                                 RICHARD A. COLLINS

Contents

Introduction

Empty your pockets or purse on a table. Chances are that among the items before you will be one or more of the following:

.... A ball-point pen inscribed with the name of a bank or insurance company.

.... A book of matches identifying a restaurant.

.... A pocket-calendar card imprinted with the name and address of a savings and loan association.

.... A key chain or key ring with an attached label naming an automobile dealer.

.... A pocket knife or flashlight received as a gift from a local hardware store and imprinted with that store's name.

.... A comb (that a salesman handed out when he introduced himself at the front door) with his company's name embossed on it.

.... A pocket protector from a gasoline service station.

.... A memo book imprinted with the name of some local firm.

.... A plastic rain cap received from a ladies' ready-to-wear shop.

.... A packet of eyeglass tissues imprinted with the name of a local optometrist.

.... An emery board, nail file, or clipper from a barber's or beautician's shop.

.... A driver's license holder stamped with the name of an automotive product or service dealer.

1

.... A packet of lipstick tissues from a neighborhood drug store or pharmacy.

Each of these products has at least one thing in common: they all represent a form of advertising that is unique in reaching the owner with a personalized message. There is, however, another feature common to all of these items: there was no obligation involved in receiving any of them; each was presented as a gift.

With this much as background, it is appropriate to consider a formal definition of the broad topic of this book, specialty advertising:

Specialty advertising is that advertising and sales promotion medium which utilizes useful articles to carry the advertiser's name and advertising message to his target audience.

This definition specifically separates "specialty advertising" from the better known "mass advertising," which is concerned chiefly with the use of television, radio, newspapers, and magazines. Specialty advertising does not necessarily compete with space or time advertising. Rather, in most instances, it *complements* other promotion by providing another method (and a very *special* one at that) of keeping the advertiser's name before the target audience. (In certain cases, of course, particularly for smaller service organizations, it is used as the sole medium to reach the market.)

To differentiate the method or system of specialty advertising from the "things" used by this medium, a more limited definition is also needed. Therefore, when talking about the products used in specialty advertising, the authors will use the term "advertising specialty" or, more simply, "ad specialty." Generally, ad specialties will be *useful* to the recipient, but this "usefulness" must be interpreted quite broadly. Some ad specialties will have a use-value as great as that of a calendar, while for others the utility may only be that of supplying a chuckle on a busy day.

The image and role of specialty advertising remains rather vague in the world of commerce, and even among professional advertising practitioners. In 1963, for instance, in a special edition of *Advertising Age* entitled "The World of Advertising," this comment was made: "There is probably no advertising medium which is more commonly used, yet less understood, than specialty advertising . . . even very few admen have more than a vague notion about this far-from-small medium."

Although this statement was made some years ago, it is still accurate, though this does not mean that educational efforts are not being made. An active specialty advertising trade association exists, and as studies are carried out on specialty advertising effectiveness, business communication activities are analyzed and related. Some clarity has resulted. As Robert C. Rollings, president of the Specialty Advertising Association International (SAAI) states:

Some of the industry endeavors to clear up the process of communications settle around semantics. Much terminology is unimportant to the user or customer, so "sales promotion," "specialty advertising," "premiums" and "gifts" are used interchangeably. But if the generation of an idea for use in marketing strategy and communications is properly identified in its functional place, the user will have a better chance to get related information, help, and more objective evaluation.

Hundreds of volumes have been written on communications, and thousands of research reports have investigated the social, psychological, philosophical, and political aspects of communications. In advertising, techniques and methods of transmitting, receiving, and creating content and form have received considerable attention. Certainly all segments of this type of business activity are related, but only the more important will be mentioned in this book. Because of the recognized growth of advertising in many areas of human endeavor, coupled with current efforts to examine more closely all of the ingredients of our marketing system and its subsystems, the authors feel that specialty advertising is one subject area deserving greater study. Current literature on specialty advertising is composed primarily of articles in trade journals, a 58-year-old monograph ("Specialty Advertising—A New Way to Build Business" by Henry Bunting), and a few special reports published by Specialty Advertising Association International, headquartered in Chicago, Illinois. Although no in-depth quantitative study was carried out for this book, it does bring together all present literature related to the topic along with interviews and questions directed to customers and members of the industry.

The authors are hopeful that this book's readers, whether practitioners, customers, or students, will approach the subject matter with an open mind as to the meaning and position of specialty advertising. To restrict any medium to its historic image, rather than openly examining its actual and potential role, is too narrow an approach. In a "systems" analysis, a blend of the optimum mix is essential. Moreover, because of the common availability of knowledge to all competitors, success in advertising often depends on the addition of a previously unused ingredient. This elusive "x" factor, sometimes demonstrated by the *innovative* use of a specialty item, can mean the difference between reaching or falling short of promotional goals.

Yet even though the authors have uncovered substantial evidence of how creative element "x" has made significant differences between this campaign and the next, the reader will find in the text persistent reference to the need to integrate *all variables* in the marketing system. What has been successfully accomplished in many marketing strategies is a matter of record. We feel more attention in the future to the proper use of specialty advertising can add further luster to successful campaign strategies.

1
Concept and role

I T would be almost impossible to find a person who hasn't received or used an advertising specialty item. The daily use of such merchandise has been increasing at a rate faster than U.S. population. Even so, misunderstanding about the role of the advertising specialty, its lack of acceptance as an important part of the total promotion mix by professional advertising people, failure to realize the full influence it can play in personal selling activities, and the inadequate significance attached to it by marketing practitioners, all suggest that specialty advertising is neither fully understood nor appreciated. Yet here is a major area of demonstrated contradiction: People who challenge the value of specialty advertising are likely to be surrounded by such items, and businessmen who profess not to be engaged in *any* advertising are generally using ad specialties.

It is important that the reader resist the temptation to conclude that specialty advertising items are insignificant novelties or trinkets used to promote a company. In the same way that magazine rate cards don't begin to tell a story about the theory of print media, neither does one ad specialty article begin to define the domain or expound the theory of specialty advertising.

Nature of the industry

As a system, specialty advertising can, and frequently does, stand alone. For instance, it is heavily used by the local small advertiser, and often his *total* budget is spent in this medium. It should not generally be looked upon as a single method, however, because it tends to be cooperative, rather than competitive, with other media.

Specialty advertising has another very characteristic feature: It can be designed to reach a very specific and controlled audience more easily than all other forms of advertising. Unlike other media that may reach millions in order to influence a specific few thousand, the ad specialty can be distributed to the precise individual the advertiser wants to reach. It can even be personalized to the individual recipient.

When using conventional media, advertisers frequently talk in terms of "cost per impression," referring to the cost of reaching one subscriber, listener, or viewer. While advertisers recognize that many of those reached are not among potential customers for their product, they do have faith that their potential customers are somewhere among those being reached. The problem lies in not knowing *what share* of those being reached are potential customers, for without such knowledge it is impossible to estimate the cost of reaching the specific potential customers. (Recently some major media analysts have employed demographic studies in an attempt to shift from mere numerical estimates.)

By contrast, the ad specialty mailing or recipient list may well be made up of *just* those persons judged to be the most likely potential customers. Utilizing such a specific target group, an advertiser is able to gauge very accurately the cost per person *reached* through his campaign. There is, therefore, good reason to believe that the specialty advertising approach can be a very economical one, providing there is a way of identifying the potential customers. As stated by Frey and Halterman in *Advertising* (4th ed.; New York, N.Y.: The Ronald Press Co., 1970, p. 49):

While the per-person cost of specialties may be comparatively high, their longer life and goodwill value may make them appropriate for special circumstances. This is particularly true in markets with easily defined parameters where the unit of sale is relatively high, where patronage extends over long periods of time, or where alternative media cannot reach prospects as economically at the appropriate time.

These observations lead to another important consideration with respect to the ad specialty: Although it is true that there is a tendency to understate the reach of a particular ad in some media because it is difficult to gauge accurately the repeat readership of a magazine or newspaper, this problem is modest compared to estimating the repeat exposures that might occur with an ad specialty item having a useful life of up to ten years. Each time the clock is consulted, the calendar referred to, the pen used—a repeat exposure to the imprinted advertising message appearing on the item has taken place. Project this situation to the literally thousands of times that these items may be used, and the difficulty of estimating the exposure to an ad specialty imprinted message can be seen. Just as in the print and broadcast media, where the degree of success of an advertisement is dependent on the theme and the execution of the message, so also the ad specialty can be more or less effective as an advertising medium depending on both the uniqueness and appropriateness of the item chosen to do the job and the taste and skill with which the product is imprinted.

To illustrate how this kind of creativity works, consider a campaign conducted by the Anaconda Aluminum Company of Louisville, Kentucky. The purpose of the promotion was to encourage the use of aluminum foil for artistic package design, along with other such applications as a mailing material. Working with a mailing list of 5,000 art directors, designers, and advertising managers of large corporations, Anaconda started the campaign with an impressive mailer entitled, "An Introduction to the Foil." The mailer contained a booklet printed on aluminum foil which explained that future mailings would demonstrate how foil could add drama and beauty to promotional printed pieces. A miniature fencing foil, with the company's name imprinted along the blade, was enclosed with the booklet. The foil (actually a letter opener) was a clever tie-in with the promotion of foil and also served as an ideal "opener" for subsequent mailings—both as a useful tool and as an interest builder. A test mailing brought an overwhelming response, as did the second mailing which announced an awards competition for achievement in aluminum foil design.

A program with a much more local slant along with an entirely different objective was carried out by a road builder, Ryan Incorporated of Janesville, Wisconsin. A school and a number of residential dwellings were located quite near Ryan's multi-million dollar construction project in Huntington, West Virginia. Extreme precaution was necessary to insure the safety of curious children. Ryan decided to inform the local community in a friendly manner that a certain amount of noise and inconvenience was inevitable. Families living near the project were invited to a buffet dinner and discussion period to acquaint them with the problems and measures necessary to insure safety. Next, the school children were guests at a Ryan-sponsored "Hot Dog Day." Each student received a white plastic hat imprinted with the company's initials. The students were also allowed—under careful supervision—to survey the construction area. School teachers cooperated by inviting children to participate in an essay contest on "How to Build a Road."

Ryan's efforts paid measurable dividends. No problems or injuries were encountered on the job site during the construction period, and a strong feeling of goodwill resulted between residents and the company. The program was so successful that Ryan has distributed hundreds of "hard hats" in similar programs near construction projects in Wisconsin and Minnesota.

One other example will help to demonstrate the diversity of objectives and methods used in specialty advertising. Controls Company of America (CCA), Heating and Air Conditioning Division, located in Milwaukee, Wisconsin, is a major supplier of controls for the automotive air conditioning industry. A promotion was needed which would make a favorable impression on top customers expected to attend a trade show and convention in Dallas, Texas. Major emphasis was placed on a hospitality suite promotion tied to a golfing theme to be called, "Dallas Hospitality Open." An imprinted golf tee attached to an invitation was mailed to a select customer list two weeks before the convention. A score card incorporated into the invitation served as a control on participation and prizes. A miniature putting green was set up in the suite, and the prize for sinking five or more holes-in-one was a three-pack of golf balls imprinted with the company's trademark. Everyone who participated received a package of four imprinted tees. CCA termed the results of the promotion "fantastic." The hospitality suite was filled beyond capacity throughout the convention while many competitors' rooms were much less well attended. A check of the score cards showed that 90 percent of those invited took part in the "Open" and favorable customer comments were received for months afterward.

Ryan's "hard hat" student promotion.

CCA's golf ball "three pack" award.

APPEALS

What are some of the advantages that specialty advertising has over other forms of promotion? First, there is certainly the benefit of personal appeal. With specialty advertising the advertiser can beam his message directly to the person he believes is the individual who buys—the decision-maker. Second, the ad specialty is directed to the sentiments or emotions of the recipient. The gift is intended to build a feeling of goodwill on the part of the receiver toward the giver. We might consider the ad specialty a form of flattery, where the advertiser is demonstrating to the person who has been presented with the gift that his patronage really counts, that he is a person held in great esteem by the promoting company.

Virtually all people like to receive gifts, and gifts are usually thought of as expressing interest, goodwill, friendship, reward—even a subtle implication of asking for cooperation from the receiver. At the same time, no overt obligation is asked as a condition for receiving the gift. Rather, a desire is built in, which it is hoped will cause the recipient to patronize the advertiser. Still, the advertiser has no guarantee of success; he can never be sure that his promotion will, in the end, culminate in a sale. No advertising or general promotion technique can provide such an assurance, of course, but with the ad specialty, there is a relatively higher level of confidence that the promotion will bring desired results.

Many advertisers have traditionally characterized specialty advertising as a form of "give away" in contrast to mass media techniques. But the question arises, "Isn't a TV or radio show free, too?" No purchase is necessary to watch a network program or to receive a newspaper where the advertisements make the printing of news financially possible. But unlike mass media, any waste associated with promotion is more visible under certain conditions in specialty advertising. (Since advertising waste has been verbalized a lot but researched very little, however, few valid statements can be made regarding waste in relation to any medium.)

The very nature of specialty advertising appeals and speaks directly to the recipient. With it, there is no need to resort to general appeals, for the medium tends to be highly selective and can be tailored to a specific target group. This dimension, of course, contains an important aspect of economy of effort, though a heavy burden is placed on the advertiser, requiring him to carefully identify and understand the common characteristics of his potential customers. The theory of market segmentation may well be applied to the use of specialty advertising. It is possible that the total potential market for a given business can be segmented into groups. While these groups may be highly homogeneous within themselves, however, they tend to be very different from one another. On this basis, the advertiser may have to design separate promotions for each of the particular groups he wants to reach. In space and broadcast advertising, this segmentation problem is being recognized more and more as a problem because these media have not generally been selective enough to permit tailoring a campaign to each group. Specialty advertising, on the other hand, is built upon this sort of emphasis and is ideally suited to carry out this type of program.

Broad use in promotion

Specialty advertising should complement and supplement a total promotional campaign. The careful planner, in creating his campaign, must be sure to prepare a many-faceted approach. It would be as much a mistake to ignore magazines and newspapers as it would be to overlook specialty advertising, for unless a general awareness of the company and its products exists prior to the use of specialty advertising, the campaign may fail in its mission simply because specialty advertising may not be able to overcome a complete ignorance of the product. Specialty advertising is concerned with ideas, not goods. The advertising specialty itself can only transmit and apply the message of the campaign; it cannot constitute the promotion in and of itself. The company that starts with the specialty advertising item and then attempts to formulate a campaign around it will probably fail in its efforts. Therefore, it follows that the ad specialty need not be new in order to be effective; instead, it must offer a good "theme-fit." Just as in any other application of advertising media, use of specialty advertising media requires a high level of originality, ingenuity, and resourcefulness. The successful specialty advertising counselor must be the same kind of creative and dynamic formulator of ideas as the advertising agency account executive.

Certain aspects of the specialty advertising industry are similar to those of other industries. The industry has staple items comprising an important part of total purchases, plus many *specialties*. According to industry spokesmen, some product differentiation is accomplished in the use of the item; this might more properly be termed a distribution differentiation. It is quite likely that companies becoming more involved in serving promotional needs will develop even more specialization of the items used. Although this text will stress the marketing aspects of promotion, the role and importance of the items themselves, that is, the medium, cannot be ignored.

Something that may trouble the reader is the similarity of the terms *advertising specialty* and *premium*. There are at least two basic differences between these terms. First, the advertising specialty is imprinted with the name and message of the advertiser, while usually the premium is not. Second, the premium is usually only obtainable after the recipient has completed some obligation, such as buying a product, sending in a coupon or box top, or at least visiting a particular business establishment. As stated earlier, the advertising specialty is always distributed free and without any (overt) obligation. Thus, a premium is a form of sales promotion; the ad specialty, an advertising method.

Estimates vary, but it is generally agreed that there are from 10,000 to 20,000 products used as advertising specialties. This multitude of products can be grouped into three major headings: (1) ad specialty items, (2) calendars, and (3) executive gifts.

There is some liberty taken in marketing literature to classify these groups. For example, in Tillman and Kirkpatrick, *Promotion— Persuasive Communication in Marketing* (Homewood, Illinois: Richard D. Irwin, Inc., 1968, p. 355), reference is made to *novelties*:

> The advertising specialty industry divides its items into executive gifts, calendars, and novelties. . . . Although there is some business use of calendars and novelties, their nature and use seem to justify their being classified and treated as ultimate consumer stimulants. Both differ from premiums in that premiums seldom carry the seller's name, and premium offers usually demand a purchase by the consumer.

The description of novelties is close to our description of ad specialties, even though there is a difference in the acceptance of such items as advertising. Tillman and Kirkpatrick describe novelties (pp. 355–57) as follows:

> Advertising novelties are not advertising according to our classifications, but the term crept in and seems likely to remain. Actually, these

novelties are gifts; they are products of value useful to and enjoyed by consumers. Usually the novelty is imprinted with the seller's name, address, and a brief promotional message. Many are kept and used over a substantial period of time. Cost may be a few pennies or a few dollars, making them resemble the modest prizes given to the least fortunate contest winners. Some occupy the consumer's wall (thermometer), some stay on the desk or table (ash tray), some stay in sewing closets (yardsticks), some are carried on the consumer's person (pens). Here are other examples:

Address book	Comb	Ruler
Key case	Litter bag	Balloon
Fan	Pencil	Knife
Paperweight	Bottle opener	Yo-Yo

As for selection, the great degrees of variety and flexibility can be inferred from the number of items available—10,000. Many of the characteristics of good premiums are equally valid here. Quality and utility must not be too low. The novelty should not be a strange, unknown item. Frequency of use is desirable over a relatively long life. Despite these, price per unit must be modest if not even low. Other selection considerations include: identity of the recipients, competitive promotional activities, our seller's promotional program, and the objective of the novelty distribution.

The big, overall objective is to build goodwill, but this breaks down into more specific jobs or goals. Here are some:

To open doors to salesmen	To recognize birthdays
To say please and thank you	To introduce salesmen
To invite	To remind
To identify prospects	To make mailings more effective
To increase distribution	To build retail traffic

Novelties must be distributed. Mail, salesmen, retailers, or advertising offers may be used. Whichever the method, the seller tries to control the distribution by preselecting his recipient group. Selective circulation means less waste; this is a significant consideration because novelties are too costly for indiscriminate circulation.

Ad specialties

Regardless of nomenclature, the ad specialty item category is the most general of the three categories, covering a broad spectrum of products that include ballpoint pens, key chains, special coins, memo pads, buttons and badges, balloons, wallets and coin purses, rain caps, and a host of other products. These products have two important characteristics in common: they are relatively inexpensive (at least in larger quantities), and they can be imprinted with an advertiser's name and advertising message. In addition, they have some utility for the recipient, ranging from emotional utility (humor, drama, nostalgia, excitement) to practical utility, as in the case of ballpoint pens and key chains. They range from actual miniatures of products to items that, ostensibly at least, are only very remotely related to the products they are expected to promote. Specialty items may well be exactly the same as products sold in stores or used as premium items, but they will invariably have a trademark, logo, or other imprint that will identify them for what they are. Typical of such items are those shown below.

In Tillman and Kirkpatrick, special emphasis is devoted to the use of matchbooks (pp. 358–59). According to their description, there

A sampling of a few well known specialty items.

are situations in which *resale matches* are often linked with some type of purchase on the part of the recipient.

MATCHBOOK PROMOTION

Approximately 15 billion matchbooks reach ultimate consumers each year, 90 percent of which are received free. Matchbooks are in the home, in the office, in the automobile, and in the consumer's pocket. Over 70 percent of all adult consumers habitually carry these books, and the adults using them use 143 books per year on the average. Three hundred thousand firms use these matches to promote a wide variety of products and services.

The typical matchbook is a packet of paper matches with a cover and a strip on which a match can be struck. Many contain 20 matches per book and are packed 2,500 books per case. Both the inside and the outside covers can carry promotional copy; these covers are used by manufacturers and retailers on both a national and a local basis.

RESALE MATCHES

One technique involves what are called resale matches; these books usually have four-color outside covers, one-color inside covers. Resale matchbooks are given away by retailers, most of whom sell tobacco products; or, they are sold by the carton in retail stores. The matchbook manufacturer sells the covers to other sellers for their promotional messages, but he controls the distribution of the matches with two limitations: the seller who buys the use of the covers can specify (1) the geographic area to which the matches go and (2) the time of year for the distribution. Resale matches can provide wide coverage at low cost because the dispensing and selling retailers stand 75 percent of the cost. These matches are frequently used by manufacturers of convenience goods.

REPRODUCTION MATCHES

Reproduction matches are designed and bought outright by the sellers who use them for promotional purposes; the sellers do not buy just the space on the covers. After adding his promotional story, the seller distributes the matches to a prechosen group or groups. Manufacturers of industrial products, makers of consumer goods, sellers of services, retailers—all are included in the group of sellers using reproduction matches. Dry cleaners, motels, and banks are prominent users. The user may dispense the matches in his own place of business, through his salesmen, or by mail. Reproduction matches are available on airlines, at banquets and meetings, in trade show booths, and at conventions.

Reproduction matches can be distinctive and unusual in various ways.

They can be personalized with each individual buyer's name or initials if the seller wants to spend that kind of money. They can be imprinted with the names and addresses of individual retailers. Circulation is under better control than is true of resale matches. The cost, of course, is higher. Inside covers are often used as coupons or as maps of the area the seller covers; they can carry lists of sales offices or show product details.

CALENDARS

The second general category of ad specialties is calendars. Overall, they represent the largest single classification in the industry's dollar volume. Literally hundreds of millions of calendars are distributed at no charge each year in this country, and, of course, many others are sold that are not used for specialty advertising purposes.

Calendars meet the need for continuity and repetition in carrying out an advertising program extremely well. The advertiser receives a high rate of return on his investment, for his message is carried daily for 365 days or more. If the unit cost of any calendar is divided by the number of days in use, the low daily cost per contact is readily apparent. Frequently this exposure is enhanced by the fact that the calendar is displayed in a very prominent location, thus providing the advertising message with preferred position.

Two surveys were conducted to determine some measure of the effectiveness and usefulness of calendars. The first study, conducted among 1,000 randomly selected businessmen in their offices, found (not surprisingly) that *all* of their offices were using calendars. In total, 8,441 calendars were found in their offices—almost 8.5 calendars per office. Of these businessmen, 87 percent said they purchased the products or services of the advertiser who supplied them with the calendars. In addition, 17.1 percent of these offices purchased additional calendars to supplement those which they had been given. The study also brought out the interesting point that 37 percent of these businessmen said that they themselves distribute their own advertising calendars.

The second study was conducted among 1,000 homeowners. In these households, 98 percent were using some type of calendar. The average incidence was 2.5 calendars per household, but 21 percent of the householders said that they needed even more, so 17 percent bought supplemental calendars. A major share of these people (64 percent) actually made a special effort to obtain calendars for use at home, and almost half (47 percent) went to a retailer to ask for a calendar. If various types of calendars had been available, these homeowners said that they would have accepted an additional 2,176 calendars. There was a high level of use of the calendars for special purposes: 81 percent of the homeowners used the calendars to record appointments and memos, and 22 percent used the calendar as a family ledger to keep track of expenditures and other household records. From an effectiveness standpoint, 2,190 advertisers of the 2,550 calendars in use were identified by the homeowner, and 77 percent of the homeowners said that they used the products or services of the advertiser. It is clear that calendars are widely accepted and used.

To avoid large distribution of calendars at one time during the year, some advertisers run their calendars from July to June, or another convenient period such as the common academic year. Certain industries will tie their calendars to a season when their representatives will be calling on the trade. These steps help to level out the production requirements for the calendar manufacturers, but even so, manufacturers must keep two years ahead of the market, anticipating public opinion, styles, and new ideas that will influence their design work for the future.

GIFTS

The third and final category of goods in the specialty advertising field is executive gifts. These are usually the more expensive items, ranging in cost from about $5 up to $25. They are given personally and selectively to businessmen and executives. Though they may be imprinted with the giver's name, generally they are not, which by strict definition would take them out of the category of specialty advertising. In such cases, a business card, note or letter may accompany the gift. These gifts are usually given in order to show appreciation or to build goodwill.

Tillman and Kirkpatrick do not consider executive gifts in the same category as calendars and ad specialties, but their description is essentially the role that is filled by this type of item (p. 320).

Executive gifts are distributed in limited quantity to important buyers, buying influences, their families, or their offices and homes. Most cost within the $10–$25 range, but some cost more. The gifts are practical and functional, many are unusual. Some are for short-run consumption— cheese, fruit, beverages, steaks, and tickets; others are for long-term use— desk sets, trays, cameras, glassware, and luggage. Although some carry the recipient's name and a few carry the seller's identification, most carry neither. Executive gifts are given in appreciation of past business and in anticipation of future business. The advertising specialty industry describes them as "reminders of a seller's thoughtfulness." Most are distributed by mail or by someone on the manufacturer's staff, perhaps a salesman. Executive gifts are, of course, received by other business buyers than retailers; they are given to such buyers as wholesalers, purchasing agents, buyers of advertising space and time—to business buyers in general.

There is nothing new in the practice of giving gifts; many instances of gift giving are recorded in the Old Testament of the Bible. Down through the centuries, gifts have been given rulers, other leaders, and business acquaintances to cement relationships and create a favorable atmosphere in which business discussions can be held.

In a recent survey conducted on the subject of business gift giving, 64 percent of the companies surveyed gave gifts and 79 percent received them. Of those giving gifts, about 88 percent also received gifts. For those who give gifts, 53 percent say they do it to say thanks to a customer or prospect, with an additional 33 percent giving gifts in order to build goodwill. Typically, they say that gift giving is a way to express appreciation, is just good business, builds closer relationships, is traditional business practice, and is done because many customers expect it. Although 39 percent say that they are sure gift giving helps build business, an additional 41 percent don't know whether it does or not. Only 14 percent believe that it does *not* build business.

There are, of course, a number of people who are vocally opposed to the idea of business gift giving, claiming that giving gifts brings about reckless competition and lack of direction in business activities. They feel that givers will inevitably try to outdo one another in both the cost and quality of the gifts. Interestingly enough, the average value of business gifts has tended to fall, rather than increase, and decisions of both who the recipient is and what the gift will be are carried out with high selectivity. In over a third of the companies giving gifts, the president or partner or owner of the business make the gift-giving decisions.

Opponents of business gift giving raise a number of additional objections. Some suggest that the companies would be better off giving the same money to charitable causes or investing it in advertising and other promotional campaigns. These people fail to realize that there is an important element of personal appeal that cannot be achieved in any logical way other than gift giving. Other antigivers feel that the time and effort devoted to arranging an effective gift program could be spent on other more valuable activities within the firm. In addition, there is always the problem of offending the person who, for some reason, has not been included on the gift list. Opponents of gift giving claim it is better to give no gifts than to run the risk of discontent. Also, after a period of time, the gift is taken for granted and is only important if it is omitted. Without considering purely moralistic approaches, there can be only one response to these points: If almost two thirds of American industry presently practice gift giving, they must feel that giving gifts has a useful and beneficial effect on their business.

Organization of the industry

The specialty advertising industry falls into three major business organization groupings: (1) suppliers, (2) distributors, and (3) direct-selling houses.

Suppliers

The supplier manufactures, imports, converts, imprints, or otherwise processes advertising specialties, calendars, or business gifts for sale through specialty advertising distributors. Estimates place the number of suppliers at somewhere between 900 and 2,500, depending upon definition and concentration of business. There are a great many other firms which act as suppliers in the advertising specialties industry, but whose primary business activities are in another industry. Suppliers tend to establish the price at which products are to be sold to ultimate customers. This does not mean, however, that price cutting is not practiced in the industry. The cut therefore tends to come out of the profit of the middleman.

The general practice in the industry is for the manufacturer to fill orders and drop-ship them to ultimate customers, an economical way to get the goods directly from producer to user. (There are exceptions to this rule in the case of the direct-selling houses and these will be described shortly.) Probably the most important factor governing the successful operation of the supplier is his ability to perform high quality imprinting on the ad specialty item. Pricing in the industry tends to follow the standard practice of quantity discounts, with prices including standard imprinting. Extra requirements such as the use of multiple colors and special tools and dies are priced individually. Discount practices vary widely according to the class of product, the price of the product, and the particular supplier, with discounts ranging from 20 to 50 percent.

The supplier makes his products known through the medium of catalog sheets, which must of necessity contain a complete sales message for the product. Frequently these catalog sheets are the distributor's only source of information regarding a particular supplier's products, though the distributor often has samples of the supplier's products that are either given to him, sold on a cost-rebate plan, sold outright, or remain the property of the supplier until paid for or returned.

It is still unfortunately true that suppliers often accept almost any individual as a distributor, often without investigation of him or further information about him. This is one factor that brings about marginal business practices in the industry.

DISTRIBUTORS

The distributor (or jobber) develops ideas for the use of specialty advertising products, buys these products from suppliers, and sells them to advertisers under his own company name. Developing advertising programs based on the effective use of advertising specialties is one of the major creative areas of the industry. Distributors tend to act as brokers, maintaining no stock of goods other than samples received from the suppliers. Because distributors often handle many lines of products produced by numerous suppliers, they generally assemble their own catalogs and direct their own selling campaigns to the business users. They tend to operate with their own business offices, office staffs, and sales force. Distributorships

range in size from one-man operations to twenty or more salesmen per sales office. As mentioned, their verified orders are sent to
the suppliers who fabricate and imprint the items and then drop-
ship the order directly to the customer, using the distributor's shipping labels. In so many words, the distributor is actually the supplier's sales force, with the sales force performing the additional
jobs of handling credit risks and making collections.

One estimate places the number of distributors in this country at
approximately 3,500, with individual sales volumes ranging from
$25,000 to millions of dollars. Often exclusive selling arrange-
ments are made between the distributor and supplier, the suppliers
then receiving the benefits of reduced possibility of price cutting,
greater knowledge of the product on the part of the selling force, and
a closer relationship between the supplier and distributor due to the
distributor handling fewer lines. With fewer accounts, the supplier
has fewer bookkeeping problems and there is the possibility that
the ad specialty may enjoy a longer life because of the increased
attention it receives from exclusive distributors. Advantages to the
distributor include fewer competitive pressures because other salesmen are not handling the same line, and the feasibility of training
salesmen in handling the lines. Also, the customer may be more
satisfied, since he is buying a product that is a relatively exclusive
one.

In order to offer the supplier reason for giving the distributor an
exclusive arrangement, the distributor should have the number and
quality of men necessary to create the volume of business expected
by the supplier. The supplier may suffer from the fact that the distributor may only adequately sell parts of the line. These problems
are similar to those faced in other industries. Although no simple
solutions to the exclusive-arrangement problems are evident, the
approach is still popular in the industry.

Direct-selling houses

Direct-selling houses combine the functions of supplier and distributor within one organization. The direct-selling house primarily
manufactures its own products and sells them directly to advertisers
through its own sales force. Basically, these organizations are large
enough to function as a total organization, successfully carrying out

the dual functions of both manufacturing and marketing, including selling. Due to complexity of product, sheer volume, or other considerations, these firms have decided to continue entirely on their own, although some use distributors in geographic locations where they do not have direct coverage.

The industry role

What is the attitude of businessmen toward firms using ad specialties in promoting their business? To test this question, an independent research firm was hired by the Specialty Advertising Association International and was directed to prepare advertisements for two hypothetical firms: a stock ad specialty for one firm and a well-designed advertisement suitable for insertion in a local newspaper or magazine for the other. The two kinds of advertising were used in order to compare the image that each approach suggested to respondent firms. Each business firm in the sample was asked six questions relating to the two hypothetical companies. Which of the two would (1) give better service, (2) be more reliable, (3) be more efficient, (4) be more up-to-date, (5) be more inviting, and (6) be more friendly? Finally, each firm was also asked "Which of these two would you patronize or recommend to a friend?" For every category, the firm using the ad specialty was rated higher, the favorable ratings running from 56 percent of the sample believing that their hypothetical firm would give better service, to a high of 78 percent that believed this firm to be more friendly. Finally, 62 percent of the sampled companies felt that they would prefer to patronize or recommend to a friend the firm using the ad specialty product. Thus, among the organizations participating in this research, the firm using the specialty advertising technique received a more favorable image evaluation. The authors felt in examining this study that although the size was limited, it was still valid in its approach.

The absolute size of the industry is still in doubt, since the industry only recently became interested in determining its relative size with respect to the overall promotional mix. A decade ago SAAI hired a public accounting firm, Ernst and Ernst, to assemble annually industry sales information from member businesses and make a projection of the total industry volume based on that information. In 1962, the first year information was available, industry sales were estimated to be $400 million, but by 1967 volume had increased to $610 million, with a 13.2 percent increase experienced between 1966 and 1967 alone. Recent estimates place total advertising expenditures for all forms of promotion at just over $20 billion, pegging specialty advertising's share of the promotional dollar at close to 4 percent. Specialty advertising, then, appears to be the fastest growing segment of all advertising, expanding four times as rapidly as the advertising field as a whole.

2

History

PRIMITIVE trade activities date back thousands of years to when men began to live in groups and concentrate on growing food. Trade routes were eventually established, and boats were used to distribute goods from the producing centers that grew and prospered. Selected products were even transported across the Alps, and others were moved by ships around the Mediterranean coast. Archeologists have uncovered evidence of organized retailing and direct selling of tools dating back 5000 years. Such methods were refined over the centuries, and by the time of the Roman Empire, division of labor in production and merchandising reached rather sophisticated levels. There was a period of regression after the Fall of Rome, however, which was finally reversed during the Crusades. Yet throughout all those many centuries, there is no single date, place or article which can be identified as the origin of advertising.

Specifically tracing the history of the specialty advertising industry is likewise not easy to do. One story, perhaps more myth than fact, is that weapon artisans in the Middle Ages gave away wooden pegs suitably inscribed with their names. These pegs were to be partially driven into a wall and used for hanging armor when it was not in use.

25

Political start

A somewhat more historically respectable account of an early use of an advertising specialty dates to 1768 when King George III of England had a likeness of himself placed on one side of a

A sample of buttons used as long as 40 years ago. Photograph through the courtesy of A. G. Trimble Company, Pittsburgh, Pennsylvania.

picture, with the inscription "In memory of the good old days," printed on the other side, his purpose apparently being to counter-act unrest resulting from activities in the American colonies. The fact that the Revolutionary War followed in just seven years tempts one to conclude that the distribution of these pictures was not totally effective in fostering goodwill.

Within the United States, one of the earliest recorded uses of advertising specialties was also associated with politics. In the Presi-dential election campaign of 1840, William Henry Harrison utilized the slogan, "Tippecanoe and Tyler too." This slogan, emphasizing Harrison's victory in the Indian Wars together with the strength of his Vice-Presidential running mate, Tyler, was printed on a variety of badges, buttons, ribbons, and posters. The campaign was highly successful, and Harrison was elected. The strategy stuck, for badges, buttons, and ribbons have played an important role in every Presi-dential campaign since 1840. For example, during the Humphrey-Nixon contest in 1968, in excess of 100 million buttons were dis-tributed by the candidates.

Practical beginning

Outside of the political arena, the first known ad specialty use in the U.S. occurred in 1845, though our country's history has, of course, recorded the colorful efforts of the Yankee peddler. He performed functions of direct selling, delivery, collections, limited sampling, and at times distributed favors with an occasional written word on them. With only a slight stretch of the imagination, these favors can be construed as specialty advertising. In 1845, however, a salesman from Auburn, New York, was having difficulty getting local busi-nessmen and shopkeepers to display his advertising signs, and to overcome their resistance, he hit upon the idea of attaching calendar pads to his signs, thus making them readily acceptable for display in homes and businesses. This salesman, whose identity has been lost, unwittingly capitalized on an axiom which is basic to the specialty advertising industry: Give the recipient a sign (representing your ad or imprint) *and* something of *value* (the calendar), and you ob-tain exposure of your message throughout the entire course of the year represented on the calendar and perhaps even beyond.

In 1869 a calendar patent was issued to George Coburn of Hartford, Connecticut. Coburn printed calendars for bankers, insurance companies, and manufacturers located in and around Hartford. The city that is looked upon as the real birthplace of the advertising specialty business in the United States, however, is Coshocton, Ohio. In that small Ohio town in 1879, Jasper I. Meek, a weekly news-

An early "pin-up" example in calendars.

paper editor, produced some of the earliest known advertising specialty items in the United States when he printed the names of local merchants on small candy boxes and burlap school bags that were then given away by those merchants.

Meek subsequently became so successful with this new business

ON OUR WAY TO

DOLD BROTHERS
General Merchandise

COPPOCK *and* MARSH

1913		JANUARY			1913	
SUN.	MON.	TUE.	WED.	THU.	FRI.	SAT.
			1	2	3	4
5	6	7	8	9	10	11
12	13	14	15	16	17	18
19	20	21	22	23	24	25
26	27	28	29	30	31	

Using the "family-home" appeal in early calendar art.

activity that he gave up his newspaper to devote himself entirely to the fledgling venture. Seeing Meek's new-found success, another Coshocton newspaper editor, H. D. Beach, abandoned his own journalistic efforts and became Meek's first competitor. These two men finally joined forces to form the Meek and Beach Company,

One of the first movie star calendar art examples.

later changing the name to the Tuscarora Advertising Company. They jointly ran the firm until 1900 when Beach left to form his own company. Meek later sold Tuscarora to the American Art Works. Coshocton, Ohio, still remains an important center for the advertising specialties business and many Coshocton firms currently produce calendars and advertising specialties. Though they are all separate companies now, in one way or another, most have some historical relationship with the original Meek and Beach Company.

Another early beginning for the specialty advertising industry occurred in Red Oak, Iowa, in 1889. Two newspapermen, Edmond Burke Osborne and Thomas D. Murphy, were copublishing the *Red Oak Independent*. The citizens of Red Oak had just voted their approval to build a new courthouse, and the *Independent* ran a reproduction of the proposed building in its pages. Osborne and Murphy hit upon the idea of getting increased mileage from the printing plate of the courthouse by printing it on bristolboard, attaching a calendar pad to this reproduction, and selling box advertisements around the picture to various local merchants. They distributed approximately 1,000 of these calendars, and a new advertising medium was launched. They later closed their newspaper and devoted themselves entirely to printing calendars. Ten years later, in 1899, Osborne quit the business, traveled to Newark, New Jersey, and established the Osborne Company.

The Osborne and Murphy Company spawned a series of firms that continue to exist in the specialty advertising industry, the most famous of these being Brown and Bigelow, now the largest firm in the industry and a division of Saxon Industries. Herbert H. Bigelow, who had been a salesman for Osborne and Murphy, in 1896 entered into a partnership with a printer, Hiram D. Brown, who, as it turned out, invested capital but never became active in the business. Sales for the first year amounted to $12,000; sales for 1970 were more than $50,000,000, and 700 full-time and 150 part-time salesmen were working for Brown and Bigelow throughout the United States and in 20 foreign countries.

During the 1880s and 1890s, ad specialty products made from cloth, metal, wood, celluloid, cardboard, and paper proliferated rapidly. Popular items during that period included imprinted buttonhooks and shoe horns, picture cards, rulers and yardsticks, pencils, and thermometers. An unusual product of the time was the horse-net, a fish-net-like shroud for horses that helped to keep off the flies! Imprinted with an advertiser's name, it became one of the first moving-sign specialties. Also during this period development in the printing art gave impetus to new types of calendars which have continued to the present as an important general item to the industry.

Association beginning

Companies of all sizes and descriptions became part of the specialty advertising industry during the late 19th century; and, inevitably, cutthroat competitive conditions, fraud, and other illegal methods became common. In addition, many firms, weakened through poor management and inadequate business methods, drifted into bankruptcy, further injuring the industry's reputation.

In order to bring stability to the specialty advertising field, a group of twelve founding companies in 1903 organized the National Association of Advertising Novelty Manufacturers, one of the earliest trade associations in the United States. A founding member described the first meeting in these illuminating and amusing words: "The chairman was the only gentleman present. At least that was my impression, for he was the only man who had the nerve to pull off his hat and coat without watching them. Every man was afraid of the other and the meeting was conducted along the lines of 'pistols and coffee for all.' Anyway, when we went home we were able to say we had met the other fellow—and we'd learned that he did not have horns." Apparently, then, the founders did not know all their competitors except by second- and third-hand reports, but nevertheless felt the need to get together to explore the possibility of some form of cooperation.

At the time of the inception of the trade association, highly competitive conditions directed many businessmen to develop unique characteristics that would provide them with a competitive edge: patents, products, properties, and individual business ideas. Successful methods were viewed as secret formulas, almost akin to possessing a map for buried treasure. Men tended to fear and avoid their competitors. Therefore, the founding of the National Association of Advertising Novelty Manufacturers was additionally significant, demonstrating as it did the progressive attitude of the founding members.

The association was formed for good and practical reasons: To educate members in order to improve business practice and to "watch legislation and inform the industry of pending matters." Certainly the influence of the scientific management era led by Taylor, Gilbreth, Gantt, and others had a strong influence on the topics discussed at many of the early annual meetings. For example, included in the eighth annual convention program (1911) were the following topics: "Cost finding, and is it desirable to have a uniform system adopted by our Association?"; "Maintaining of our prices with particular reference to competitors who make foolish prices, either in ignorance or vengefulness"; "A simple, consistent symmetrical system for determining the cost of production, based on fundamental principles of the science of cost finding."

The dual but interrelated problems of pricing and cost determination were significant problems in the association's early years. As one member put it, "The 'one-price' system for selling merchandise was of much later origin. Up until 1905 and thereabouts, the typical seller of merchandise, particularly in this industry, was out to make a sale at the highest price possible, but if the higher price was not possible, then he endeavored to make the deal at a lower price." Price lists were few, and instances of their use were far between.

Very few companies had any real knowledge of costs, and even those who did would not let such considerations control the price at which goods were sold. While the members could not agree on a uniform cost system, the discussions were of considerable benefit to those members who had no cost systems, for they had the opportunity to see what they ought to have in order to operate profitably.

Much discussion during the annual meetings was centered around a very practical and mutually beneficial subject—developing and publishing a listing of exclusive, nonexclusive, and ex-salesmen of all the member companies. These lists were to be used as an aid to members who were considering hiring a particular salesman. If a man had worked for another company, the hiring firm could check with his previous employer to determine whether the salesman's work had been satisfactory and under what conditions he had separated from his previous job. Such lists continued until the early 1920s when they were discontinued due to sheer volume, with thousands of names appearing on the "ex-salesmen lists," but only hundreds on the "active salesmen lists."

Ex-salesmen's lists were not used to blackball these men (although at times this probably did occur) but to protect a manufacturer from being cheated by new salesmen who would accept expensive samples, travel expense, and training and then depart, never to be heard from again. Another popular technique among dishonest salesmen at the time was to send fictitious orders to the manufacturer, who would immediately remit a commission check to the salesman, who would then promptly disappear, check in hand!

ASSOCIATION DEVELOPMENT

Another issue that the association became heavily involved with during the late 1920s was the burning question of calendar reform. Advocates of reform urged a 13-month calendar, with every month consisting of 4 weeks or 28 days. Thus every month of any year would begin on the same day. The 365th day (13 months of 28 days equals only 364 days) would be a holiday at the end of the 13th month. In opposing calendar reform, the association was pitted against a very formidable collection of well-known businessmen including Pierre S. DuPont of the DuPont Company, William Wrigley of the Wrigley Gum Company, and E. M. Stattler of Armour and Company.

The reformers were led by a man who was willing to put significant time and money into the project, George Eastman of the Eastman Kodak Company. The association, led by its calendar manufacturer contingent, conducted a very active campaign against reform, contending that the population in general would be opposed, chiefly on the basis of sentiment. "What," they asked, "will happen to the dates we all hold dear—birthdays, anniversaries, the Fourth of July, and other national holidays?" In addition, the question of superstition was brought up about the number 13—would this also be a significant barrier to revision? Since reform would have lessened the need for the annual appearance of new calendars as we have them today, a business threat *did* face the manufacturers, although it may not have been as great as they imagined. Much to their satisfaction, reform was defeated, not only in this country but in the League of Nations.

One of the major activities of the industry's trade association over the years has been its legislative work. Through its efforts, such matters as increased postal rates, adverse taxes, barriers to certain forms of advertising, and other proposed legislation that would have

been detrimental to the association's members have been successfully fought and defeated. Using this work as a measure of its effectiveness, the association has done much to create a business climate
in which its members can work and prosper.

Through the 1910s, 1920s, and 1930s, the association continued
to grow and bring about changes. Innovation was one of the problems that faced the emerging industry, but for specialty advertising
the problem had a sort of reverse twist. Where other industries had
to strive constantly just to bring about a minimum level of innovation, innovation was the name of the game in specialty advertising.
This was so much so that industry products were called by a new
term, *novelties*. As Webster defines it, a *novelty* is "something new
or unusual—the quality or state of being novel—a small manufactured article intended mainly for personal or household adorn-
ment." What is especially important about this definition is that there
is certainly *no* suggestion of something made cheaply—that is, items
that would be referred to as junk or gimmicks by the general public.
It is true that the products were designed to be manufactured inex-
pensively enough so that companies could afford to give them away.
Naturally, then, it was inevitable that some products would be less
adequately designed and built than others, and so it follows that some
novelties *were* poorly enough built to cause the public to jump to the
conclusion that *all* ad specialties were of cheap quality.

Because of this problem, the association early in its existence decided to review its name, eliminating the word "novelty," and re-
placing it with the phrase "advertising specialty." Since 1915 this
phrase has in one form or another appeared in the official name of
the trade association.

At the same time, an image was being established with respect
to the sales personnel in specialty advertising. Too often, the salesman for advertising specialties seemed to exhibit the attitude that
he was prepared to serve essentially as an agent to get the customer
"whatever he wants," and was often thought of in terms of an agent
carrying a suitcase full of catalogs which contained all the small
merchandise items known to man, or so it seemed. (This order-
taker image of the salesman existed not only in the advertising specialties business—witness the message conveyed by the character
Willie Loman in Arthur Miller's *Death of a Salesman*.) Also, in
order to gain rapid representation, many of the fledgling manufacturing firms in the industry hired full-time men with no ex-

perience or salesmen who would serve their lines only part-time. Such representation was too frequently known for its high pressure tactics, fast talk, and quick sales. On many occasions the individual client was not properly served with products tailored to his needs and problems. Instead, the easiest sale was made. Products were sold that too often did not adequately or effectively serve the needs of the client. Thus, inadequate sales representatives also played a detrimental part in the industry's early reputation.

A third problem that existed resided in basic economic principles. One of the factors associated with highly competitive conditions in an industry is a lack of barriers to entry—barriers such as high technological skill or high capital investment. This was true in the advertising specialty industry, where these barriers are only very low hurdles. Technology is often at the level of punch-press parts, injection molding, and high speed printing. Most of the products are easily duplicated and are generally not patented—patent procedures often take longer than the potential life of the product. Capital requirements are also often low, for the dual reasons that the equipment is generally not that expensive and much of the work can be subcontracted to other companies. Thus, very little exists to prevent fly-by-night firms from entering the industry at will.

Historical fragmentation

Specialty advertising, in its infant stages, included many products beyond the executive gifts, calendars, and imprinted items that now constitute the industry. One of the categories that now exists separately is outdoor advertising. Because of the knowledge of printing and design available in the industry, it was logical that advertising specialty firms were among the first to prepare signs to be placed along road right-of-ways to encourage passersby to use various products and services. Initially these signs were of modest size, and only later in their evolution did they begin to incorporate illustrations and various forms of lighting and design to make them noticed and read.

Because this form of advertising became more and more specialized, the outdoor advertising industry branched off and became a separate field all to itself. Closely tied to the origin of the outdoor advertising industry in the ad specialties family were the display cards, labels, posters, and banners which have been later separated into the so-called "point-of-purchase" advertising materials industry. For the same reasons—knowledge of printing and design—this business had its start as a part of the ad specialty industry. Once again the unique demands of this fledgling advertising activity enabled it to separate and become yet another element of the promotional mix.

The industry as a whole was highly self-conscious about its image among businessmen in general and advertising agencies in particular. To overcome general business resistance, the association prepared and distributed handbooks and brochures that presented the specialty advertising story to businessmen and the academic community. This started as early as 1915 when members of the industry financed their first educational booklet, "The Dollars and Cents Value of Advertising Specialties." The pamphlet was prepared and distributed to schools, students, businesses, and other organizations to improve the image of the industry and educate the public about specialty advertising. This first booklet was followed by another, more complete and this time sponsored by the trade association itself, called "Why—How—When—Where You Should Use Specialty Advertising." Unfortunately, much of this material was designed for hard sell and not to persuade, educate, or inform. It appears that these early efforts had little effect. On the other hand, another approach to creating favorable goodwill was attempted in 1923 when funds were raised from the members to develop a two-reel motion picture called "Secrets of Success." This film was widely shown to service clubs, chambers of commerce, and other organizations of businessmen with apparently greater success. Another film was made in 1925, but it did not have the same impact as the first. Because of the great depression of the 1930s and only the limited beneficial effect of both the movies and booklets, the industry did little else in an image-building direction until after 1945.

Finding a niche

The industry's relations with advertising agencies has always been a major concern. As early as 1908, the annual convention proceedings contained comments by members lamenting the fact that a poor and generally unsatisfactory relationship existed between the agencies and advertising specialty companies. It was thought at the time that this problem stemmed from the industry being identified by the term *novelties.* It appears, however, that the major barriers to an improved relationship sprang out of two difficulties. First, there was the problem of compensation for the agency. In many cases no single arrangement was clearly developed to pay the agency its standard 15 percent commission. Beyond this, the amount of dollars allocated for ad specialties was generally only a small portion of an advertiser's total promotional budget. The agency thus often felt that for the amount of income involved too much effort was needed to work out an ad specialty program.

The second difficulty goes back to the novelties problem. The agency man tended to look upon ad specialties as "beneath his dignity" and associated the average ad specialty salesman with the peddler, a man armed with a case of catalogs and covering first all the businesses on one side of Main Street, then on the other. The agency executive saw the ad specialty salesman as unprofessional and unsophisticated, reliable enough to process an order but not capable of acting as a part of the promotional team in solving a client's problem. That the industry recognized this problem and took action to overcome it (a point to be more fully discussed in later chapters) was of course vital.

From its earliest beginnings, the industry struggled to legitimize itself as a part of the promotional mix used by well-managed business firms. An interesting and colorful participant in this struggle was Dr. Henry S. Bunting, who started publishing a monthly periodical called *Novelty News* in Chicago in 1901, two years prior to the formation of the trade association itself. By virtue of his publication, personal interest, and enthusiasm, he became a kind of ex-officio member of the association and contributed his ideas often and at length at the early conventions. He was a sort of theoretician for the industry, acting as a spokesman for it before other groups. (In many ways, his publication performed a service to the industry not too dissimilar to that now performed by *The Counselor,* a matter discussed below in more detail.) Dr. Bunting was a prolific writer and devoted many of his literary efforts to subjects that he described as "books of business economics."

One of Bunting's books, *Specialty Advertising—The New Way to Build Business,* was published in 1914 and is the first known publication written specifically on the subject. Some of his analyses of the industry demonstrate outstanding insight into the theoretical aspects of the field, as well as being highly useful in describing the composition and orientation of the industry at that time. A number of his viewpoints have been adopted or have influenced the writing of this book, since they are still pertinent today.

One of the most recent episodes in the history of the industry was the power struggle of the 1950s. The trade association, by then known as the Specialty Advertising National Association, had to many become simply the instrument of the older, more conservative members of the industry. This association was, additionally, strongly dominated by the manufacturers and thus was more concerned with production- and legislation-oriented problems than with marketing problems. As a result, a competitive organization developed, the Advertising Specialty Guild of America. Formed in 1953, this new association tended to concentrate its attention on sales and marketing problems. That such an orientation was badly needed is clearly demonstrated by the fact that within a year, it had more members than the Specialty Advertising National Association.

ADVERTISING SPECIALTY INSTITUTE

An important part of the industry is the Advertising Specialty Institute (ASI), a division of National Business Services, Inc., which publishes *The Counselor,* the industry's trade journal. Unlike the Specialty Advertising Association International, the nonprofit trade association, ASI, is a business corporation organized to produce a profit. As such, it has no members, but has developed an extensive group of subscribers. In addition to publishing *The Counselor,* it acts as an information service organization for both suppliers and distributors. Suppliers, for example, are sold an ASI distributor rating service. They are not, however, bound or committed to use this information in dealing with distributors. A fixed set of criteria are used, primarily centered around tangible evidence of having done business with ten ASI listed suppliers. No financial reports are required from distributors, although they are requested to submit financial information twice a year. Cooperation is almost universal, and ASI then has this information checked by a third party.

An ASI information sheet specifically includes: distributor ID number; complete company name and address; name of principal executive; organization code (proprietorship, partnership, or corporation); year established; territory covered (from local to national or international); location (store, plant, office building, or residence); broad description of operations (18 classifications); estimated annual sales (classifications from under $10,000 to over $500,000); estimated net worth (classifications from under $5,000 to over $500,000); sales force size at busiest period; audit information regarding discounting and remittance records (established every six months by checking with suppliers); and, a symbol of change or addition since the last weekly report.

This is a far cry from the initial efforts of the ASI founders 20 years ago when the first edition of the *Register* was released. That was simply a list of names, addresses, and brief descriptions of manufacturers' lines and geographical listings of jobbers. In 1954 *The Counselor* was initiated, designed exclusively for the advertising specialty industry, offering challenging concepts along with news, broad observations about other areas of promotion, and ads about new products.

ASI likewise provides services to distributors. A *magni-file* is sold to them which is a miniaturization of a large number of catalog sheets provided by suppliers. The 1970–71 issue combined and reduced a total of 12,800 catalog pages, with over 50,000 items in 900 different product lines. Suppliers, product specifications, and prices are given, plus an index for proper information location. Franchised suppliers are identified, and a special magni-view finder reading device is available for distributors to use in their own selling efforts.

Another item ASI makes available to distributors is the *Consolidated Catalog,* which is published in three volumes according to the price range of the items included. Approximately 1500 pages contain complete ordering information for each of the items mentioned, identifying sources by coded supplier numbers. The *Advertising Specialty Registry,* a cross-reference trade directory, also using a supplier number coding system, likewise helps distributors identify those suppliers actively engaged in servicing distributors. This is kept current from information provided by hundreds of distributors throughout the industry.

Recent industry steps

Realizing that the success of a changing industry is partly dependent upon its unity, the two previously mentioned associations began consolidation attempts in 1956. The ultimate combination of those two groups, however, did not take place until 1963. During the intervening years, both organizations improved, each taking on characteristics of the other until, at the time of consolidation, their philosophies and points of view were closely aligned with one another.

The new organization, today called the Specialty Advertising Association International (SAAI), has among its objectives the obtaining of a greater share of the advertising dollar. It was also organized "to promote the welfare of its members and the Specialty Advertising Industry in general; to improve the industry's services to the general public and to cooperate with officials of governmental agencies; to further the acceptance of specialty advertising as an advertising medium; to advance the calibre and efficiency of specialty advertising salesmen and to conduct research, compile statistics, publish reports and disseminate other useful information to its members."

The association has done much in recent years to improve both the image of specialty advertising and the quality of the industry's sales personnel. One of the first projects of the combined group was to obtain professional public relations assistance in carrying out its program. Another decision involved continuation of the annual executive development seminars for industry personnel. These are designed to foster an understanding of the marketing orientation among managers and future managers of the industry's members. In addition, regional sales training clinics have been held in a number of areas throughout the United States. To enhance the industry's image among businessmen, the association holds an annual Specialty Advertising Awards Competition, recognizing excellence in application by both the specialty agency and its client. Finally, the association has a SAAI Speaker's Bureau which provides speakers and material to any interested organization. Through these and other efforts, the industry has accomplished much in the way of changing and improving its image and in providing itself with an increasingly recognized position as a part of American industry's promotional mix.

The association has likewise recently released a 16-mm color film entitled "The Lasting Medium," which was designed primarily to relate the role of specialty advertising to sales and marketing groups at professional and university levels. The three major categories—specialties, calendars, and gifts—are explained with brief case histories in a problem-solving relationship. Association leaders expect the film to carry the general message of the medium to marketing influencers and decision makers as well as to personnel of the suppliers and distributors.

3

The marketing/ promotional mix

THUS far we have introduced the general subject of specialty advertising and have covered the history and development of the industry. The fact has already been stressed that, because specialty advertising is used in conjunction with a number of other marketing efforts, it becomes an integral part of the overall marketing scheme of things. In this context, then, it is important to examine more closely the interrelationship of all the factors of marketing and to demonstrate how specialty advertising functions as a complementary and supplemental part of the total approach to marketing. Attention is therefore directed to the consideration of certain parts of marketing theory, and ultimately to how specialty advertising plays its role as part of a total marketing system.

Marketing concept

Almost all major U.S. business firms claim to subscribe to the philosophy of the marketing concept. There are two fundamental ideas that underlie the concept: first, consumer orientation is critically important, becoming the basis of all company planning, policies, and operations; second, profitability, rather than sheer sales volume, should be the longer-range financial focus of the firm.

To a large degree when discussing "marketing concept" one is actually concerned with a philosophy of business. It is an overall guiding direction, a school of thought, or the approach a business should take as it adjusts its assets and talents to the competitive environment. This concept is certainly not new. Adam Smith, for example, mentioned that the end purpose of all production should be consumption. The current version of the marketing concept puts added emphasis on a long-range viewpoint, the consumer or user having a more influential role than formerly in decisions about which products and services are to be created. Furthermore, this business philosophy is not confined to any industry or company, regardless of size or location.

Some writers in discussing the concept tend to demean the role of selling. A more valid approach would be to add dimensions to direct selling, not to reduce the importance of the sales function. It is further necessary to point out that for a company to embrace the marketing concept by name or organizational structure only, is ultimately a waste. Becoming marketing-oriented means acceptance and implementation of this business philosophy, not merely giving it lip service.

In *Marketing Management,* by Field, Douglas, and Tarpey (Columbus, Ohio: Charles E. Merrill Books, Inc., 1966, p. 15) six characteristics of a marketing-oriented management are listed:

1. Management is growth-minded. Among other things, this means that management believes in the principle of creative adaptation to social, economic, and political change.
2. Management has a long-range view of such things as new products, institutional advertising, sales training, rather than a short-run view. (Some new policies that improve the long-range profitability may result in temporary declines, as a number of companies have discovered; but the insecure "sales-minded" management looks only for immediate results and is intolerant of the long-run improvement.)
3. Management stresses the mutual interdependence of all elements in the organization. Emphasis is placed on cooperation, coordination, and planning.
4. Management is research-oriented and constantly seeks to find new market opportunities and to avoid product provincialism.
5. Management defines its products in terms of the utility they have for the users.
6. Management is primarily concerned with consumer satisfaction and

believes that volume and profits are a necessary result of quality products at fair prices.

The authors further point out (p. 16) nine economic factors leading to the adoption of the marketing concept:

1. Increased plant capacity and automation have eliminated production as a major economic problem and have substituted the problem of over-capacity or under-consumption.
2. Increased competition from new products and foreign-made goods has accentuated the need for more effective marketing.
3. Product diversification and scrambled merchandising have produced "crisis-cross competition" for the consumer's discretionary dollar, so that color television now competes with the second car.
4. Consumer affluence, full employment, job security, and discretionary purchasing power have made mass marketing possible and necessary.
5. Growing consumer education and product information have made sophisticated marketing necessary.
6. The growth of consumer credit has stimulated consumer buying in certain lines, particularly more expensive purchases (cars, appliances, travel) and at the same time has increased consumer freedom to shop around.
7. Large long-term capital investments in plant, machinery, and Research and Development have intensified competition and the need for effective marketing in order to protect these investments.
8. More sophisticated managements have increased competition through improved management methods resulting in greater productivity, lower costs, and more effective marketing.
9. Because the United States has a growth-oriented economy and a national policy of full employment, better marketing is necessary.

Since the individual firm is a part of an industry which in turn is part of the total economic activity, a broad view must be taken in considering the marketing concept. This text concentrates on one segment of the promotional mix, but it would be incorrect not to acknowledge the environmental umbrella under which all marketing functions exist, including social, economic, political, technical, and ethical phenomena. One must also be cognizant of the increased segmentation of groups previously seen as homogeneous. This is due in part to growth and in part to the overt discarding of preceding behavior patterns by larger numbers of people, resulting in new miniature or mini-markets as significant classifications. Although social status and population mobility factors are important in such changes, perhaps even more important is greater knowledge on the part of the American consumer. Today people realize that there are virtually unlimited alternatives to living patterns. Innovation and change have—at least for the moment—become normal, and this trend has carried into the area of business methods and practices.

The marketing concept gained acceptance in response to the problems existing among business organizations which grew too large to be guided by the interest and direction of a single compact group of owners. Such complex organizations found themselves increasingly out of touch with the ultimate consumer, making it more and more difficult to communicate with him. Because under such circumstances no single entrepreneurial focus exists in a firm, programs often fragment themselves into vested-interest activities of individual functional areas. It is not unusual to find departments within a firm working at cross-purposes.

To solve this problem, the marketing concept emphasizes the idea of total consumer orientation, with the result that the firm becomes skillful at understanding and directing the business to do what suits the capacities of the company. In earlier times, the entrepreneur himself set corporate objectives and then saw to it that they were achieved. The marketing concept provides a way for firms to develop a whole new planning process centered on the consumer's wants and desires, thus attempting to return to a flexibility not unlike that of the small shop owner who can immediately change policy in response to complaints or requests.

In subscribing to the marketing concept, a firm, in a sense, becomes one vast marketing organization, with the chief executive of that firm functioning as the primary marketing executive, literally, if not in fact.

Marketing mix

Another important part of marketing theory that has profound influence over the use of specialty advertising is the fundamental idea of the *marketing mix,* a term coined by Neil H. Borden of the Harvard Graduate School of Business. In his work relating to advertising and promotion, Borden realized that different overall strategies might be employed by the firm in bringing about a profitable operation in the light of circumstances faced by that firm's management. He recognized that advertising was only one element to be considered in the overall strategy of a marketing program. In looking for a way of more adequately stating this concept of the balancing of elements, Borden was inspired by the work of an associate of his who had described the business executive as a

"decider," an "artist;" . . . a "mixer of ingredients," who sometimes follows a recipe prepared by others, sometimes prepares his own recipe as he goes along, sometimes adapts a recipe to the ingredients immediately available, and sometimes experiments with or invents ingredients no one else has tried (New York, N.Y.: Advertising Research Foundation, Inc. *Journal of Advertising Research,* Vol. 4, No. 2, June 1964, p. 2).

Thus if the businessman functioned as a mixer of ingredients, it became logical that he was designing a marketing mix.

A reasonable next step in the presentation of this idea of the marketing mix was to list and evaluate the elements that might be included in this mix. Borden's original list was quite extensive, but current writers have reduced his extensive listing of elements to five major considerations. They are classified under the general headings of (1) product policy, (2) price policy, (3) channel of distribution selection, (4) logistics, and (5) promotions. These variables become the working tools that the marketing manager uses in his response to the ever-changing marketing process. The marketer must continue to look at his products and markets, building a program which will allow him to attract the best number of customers for his planned scale of operations.

The marketing mix and promotional objectives

To understand specialty advertising in the marketing mix, some attention must be directed to objectives. Objectives become the strategy portion of promotional planning; the tasks becoming all more tactical in nature. A wide variety of tasks tend to be related to the audience one is trying to reach. Much of promotion is directed toward the ultimate purchaser himself, whether that person is a consumer or industrial user. On the other hand, the promotion may be designed to reach the middleman whose efforts are involved with the distribution of the product. An excellent list of product advertising objectives or tasks is provided in the text, *Introduction to Marketing Management: Text and Cases,* by Rewoldt, Scott, and Warshaw (Homewood, Illinois: Richard D. Irwin, Inc., 1969, p. 387):

1. Promote the sale of a manufacturer's or producer's brand through present retail dealers
   a) by getting new customers to buy, and
   b) by getting present customers to buy more of the product than in the past.
2. To assist in the sale of a branded product by giving consumers the names and addresses of the selected retailers who carry the item.
3. Where products are sold house-to-house, to help sell the brand
   a) by paving the way for the salesmen, and
   b) by getting leads for the salesmen to follow up.
4. To help get distribution for a new product, or extend the distribution of an old product
   a) by creating a demand at retail stores through consumer advertising, and
   b) by stimulating interest of retailers in the product through advertising directed to them.
5. To encourage retailers to display, advertise, and sell the product actively
   a) by telling them through advertising of the opportunity for increasing profit through such activity, and
   b) by informing them of the manufacturer's promotional plans and encouraging them to capitalize on such effort through tie-in promotion.
6. To expand the sales of an industry, or to counteract an adverse sales trend
   a) by advertising sponsored by a group of competing manufacturers or producers.

Note also that advertising created to carry out any of these tasks must of course relate to the product's life-cycle. During the beginning stages of this life-cycle, promotion will be aimed at creating *primary* demand for the product. In this phase of the effort, the theme will tend to emphasize general desire for the product category, rather than for a particular brand. Later in the life-cycle, effort will be redirected to promotion for a brand of an individual manufacturer. This latter effort is directed toward increasing market-share, rather than to increasing demand for the product category as a whole. This type of demand is often referred to as *selective* demand.

It is not surprising that some disagreement has developed among both marketing theorists and practitioners as to where attention and emphasis should be concentrated. This is due in part to the inherent difficulty of identifying the costs of some activities as necessary either to successful distribution or promotion and merchandising. It has been suggested that a firm's marketing mix include all activities engaged in to promote the actual sale of its products. This not only refers to the allocation of financial resources among specific activities, but also within each activity as to just how, where, and when funds are spent. These are the qualitative aspects of the mix. It's obvious, therefore, that the development of a marketing mix is a complex and dynamic arrangement of variables.

MARKETING MIX IN PRACTICE

Several approaches to developing a workable mix have been made. Alfred R. Oxenfeldt in *Executive Action in Marketing* (Belmont, California: Wadsworth Publishing Company, Inc., 1966) lists various steps to consider in evolving the process. For a complete discussion, the reader is directed to this source. There does seem to be a pattern of approach, however, which follows these steps:

1. The chief marketing executive mobilizes his company's resources to achieve the attainable objectives his top management has identified, selected and communicated.

2. The marketing department is charged with the responsibility of managing all tools and skills to create and serve the identified customer-mix.

3. According to variations of industries and firms, and within the individual company limitations associated with finances, image and role, talents and capacities, competition and customer-mix, policies must be established to deal with products, pricing, channels, direct selling, advertising and promotion, services, and the structure to manage all components.

4. Budgets and controls are essential, with both quantitative and qualitative factors used to determine progress and accomplishment.

In doing this, marketing management must necessarily evolve alternatives to various decisions and approaches. This can eventually be thought of as "back-up systems." Whenever feasible, tests should be employed to help in determining the value of one approach over another. The true value may well be the best *combination* of efforts that is possible.

5. An essential base of all strategy (and one often neglected) involves decisions about time and timing. Questions to be considered are:

a)   How long will present marketing conditions prevail?

b)   How soon can the company expect to see results?

c)   How soon will competition react?

d)   What happens if time expectations are not met?

e)   Is short range strategy likely to overlap with long range goals?

f)   Has an expected product or service life-cycle been established?

g)   What flexibility exists in the company's timing strategy?

Systems and subsystems.   A firm's marketing operation must recognize that it should be working toward the overall objective of uniting each element into an organized and integrated program of action. In the long run, the corporation's goal is to maximize return on investment, which requires the most profitable allocation of company resources. Although each variable contributes its own unique share to this overall objective, to a great extent the firm faces the problem of suboptimization, so often recognized in systems analysis. To overcome this, not only must the firm try to maximize the effectiveness of each variable, but it must also work toward the total integration of these variables to benefit from the synergistic effect that can be gained through such coordination.

Each of these parts of total marketing policy also clearly contains a submix of elements that must be coordinated with the broader program. Because the firm will usually produce more than one product or product line, we might refer to the complete product line as the *product mix*. In similar fashion, there will be a mix within each of the other major elements.

Product policy.   The firm must design and market products which both satisfy the needs and interests of the buyers, as well as adapt to the internal and external environment which the company faces. Major considerations that the firm must be aware of include not only the state of competition and their product offerings, but also various legal barriers prohibiting certain practices and the estimated probability that the product will face an adequate level of demand for sufficient profitability throughout the product's life cycle. In addition, a number of internal factors enter into a decision relating to products, such as available production facilities, managerial ability, financial capability, and other dimensions that are a part of product-planning process.

The firm must see that in today's dynamic market there is no such thing as a stable, irreplaceable product or service; therefore each firm must be continually on the alert to seize every opportunity that presents itself in whatever way is most feasible. For example, at one time, firms holding a patent on a unique and desirable product were judged to be in business forever. Today, technology is changing so fast that patent protection is of limited value in insuring tomorrow's business.

Pricing policy. From the company's internal point of view, the firm must price its products in such a way as to receive an acceptable return on the investment At the same time, however, the price that the business firm selects must provide the consumer with sufficient expected satisfaction to equal the amount of money he has to pay for it. Such a price balance is not static, but tends to change over time due to changes in consumer preferences, which are in turn altered by fashion trends and social, economic, and political changes. Along with these influences, new products are constantly being introduced by competitors that may in themselves have a profound effect on consumer preferences. Thus, as satisfactions shift, new equilibrium points must be reached between satisfaction and costs that are evidenced by price changes.

In addition to the points already mentioned, the firm also faces restrictions imposed through marketing law. Both the Robinson-Patman Act and the Federal Trade Commission Act, among others, provide tight restraints on a firm's liberty in pricing its products. Price may also be affected by unusual pricing conditions that exist within an industry or a geographic region. A price change by a leader within an industry is almost certain to be matched by others, and a price war can be an ever-present danger. All of these conditions interact with the company's policy, as well as corporate non-marketing resources that influence the company's expected return on investment.

Channel policy.   Selection of the channel of distribution can be an extremely critical and far-reaching decision for the firm. Such factors as consumer buying habits, shifts in population concentration affecting the location of the market, and the various kinds of institutions available to carry out the plan for distribution must all be taken into account. Typically, the manufacturer chooses between selling to the consumer directly or through some arrangement of middlemen. The decision is affected by considerations relating to the market, the product, and the company itself.

One market factor to consider is whether the product is primarily a consumer product or an industrial product. No retailers are needed if the product is designed to be used in the production of other goods. Another point to consider is the number of potential customers: the greater the number, the more likely it is that the firm will use middlemen to give the product greater distribution. Geographic dispersion has a similar bearing on distribution: the more concentrated the market, the less likely it is that the firm will have to use wholesalers and other agent middlemen. Order size and customer buying habits will also influence the company's channel choice.

From a product point of view, the unit value of the product tends to dictate the funds available for distribution. Usually, the lower the unit value of a product, the longer the channel of distribution. Additionally, the product's physical characteristics are also quite important. If the product tends to be bulky, perishable, technical in nature, or customized for a particular user, the producing firm will be more likely to use a shorter channel. Finally, the extent of the product line also affects channel choice; the more complete the line, the more feasible it is for the firm to serve its market directly than through middlemen.

Company considerations also have their effects on channel choice. Here such elements as reputation of the company, financial resources, experience and ability of management, and desire for control of the channel become very important. Serving customers directly tends to require moderate to high levels of all of these elements. In addition, any services that only the manufacturer can render can also be so important that the company may be forced to select a direct channel.

The next major variable of the marketing mix to consider is

logistics. Briefly defined, logistics affects time and place utility in goods and services. Place utility is achieved primarily through the use of transportation in facilitating movement of the goods. Time utility is brought about through both the storage of goods and the availability of services. The overall objective of logistics is to provide the correct variety of goods to middlemen at the proper time and at a cost acceptable and in line with customer service requirements. To do this, careful control must be exercised in using such components as transportation, inventory control, warehousing, and supply scheduling.

Promotion policy.   The final variable of the marketing mix is promotion. No matter how good a product or service may be, the businessman must recognize that he must stimulate the potential customer to action through some part of a promotional program. In essence, a firm uses promotion to inform the general public how its products differ from those of its competitors and also to announce most effectively the introduction of new products. To accomplish these purposes, the firm selects an appropriate blend of promotional forces. These forces consist of face-to-face presentation of sales messages in the form of personal selling, communication of sales messages through advertising, and the supporting promotional activities of sales promotion. This is the most advantageous use of the promotional mix.

Promotion is also a function of imperfect competition. It is used by a firm to demonstrate its product differentiation, its ability to utilize the condition of imperfect competition, and its ability to capitalize on the fact that there is less than complete market information. Communication is a major part of promotion, suggesting the desire of a firm to send a message to a receiver in an effort to share an idea, attitude, or some other kind of information. Thus, promotion's major efforts are in the direction of creating a message (equivalent to encoding the information) and finding a target at which to aim the message and a medium through which to convey it.

One of the major decisions to be made in the use of promotion is dividing the mass of the population into a group of prospects or a net group of nonusers. Carrying out this separation requires a knowledge of customer characteristics. This same knowledge is of great assistance in selecting the targets of promotional efforts. When a firm is using middlemen in their channel of distribution, it will consider three major approaches in making its promotional decisions:

1. Should it attempt to *push* its products through the channel by aiming the promotion mainly at the middlemen who will then sell to final customers?

2. Would it be better to *pull* the product through the channel by aiming its promotion at the final user and thus creating demand for the product through the channel?

3. Perhaps a combination of the push and pull methods ought to be used. Though more expensive, totally it may be more effective and work more rapidly.

Timing the promotional effort is also of critical importance. A number of considerations may have bearing on timing, such as competitors' promotion programs, company plans relating to new models and products, and the seasonal sales patterns of the company's products. If a firm is manufacturing Christmas-tree lights, it must recognize that a May promotion will have little effect or benefit on its sales success in December (unless the promotion is aimed at the middlemen, who tend to order their Christmas goods at that time of year). If companies in an industry traditionally take orders for a substantial share of their volume at a national trade show, a company cannot afford to miss that show.

The nature of the market itself is as important to promotion as it is to the choice of a distribution system. If its market is limited geographically, a firm will tend to use promotional ingredients quite different from those used to reach a nationally distributed market. In the local market, personal selling may be the most useful promotional device; in the national market, major media advertising may be far more effective. The nature of the market may also be expressed through the concentration of customers. In both industries and markets where a heavy concentration exists, personal selling will very likely be the prime consideration.

Another important consideration relates to the nature of the product itself. For consumer goods, whether the product is considered a convenience, shopping, or specialty item will have an important effect on the promotional choice made by the company. For example, a firm marketing a convenience good will likely place heavy reliance on its own national advertising plus an emphasis on point-of-purchase display materials. With regard to industrial goods, the classification of the product as being an installation, raw material, fabricating supply, accessory equipment, or operating supply affects the promotional choice in a similar way. Installations, for instance, will probably receive almost exclusive emphasis on personal selling.

Finally, the stage of the product's life-cycle will also bear on the choice of its promotional mix. In the introductory stage for a new product, emphasis can be placed on personal selling in order to inform the prospect that the product exists, how it is used, and what forms of want-satisfaction benefits it can be expected to deliver. In the middle period of the product's life, manufacturers tend to shift an increasing emphasis to advertising. Because most consumers are already aware of the product at this stage, advertising tends to work more heavily in the direction of persuasion, rather than information only. In the final stages of the product life-cycle, promotional efforts are often curtailed to a very low level, with the major promotional effort reserved for the next new product.

TECHNIQUES

Within the general category of promotion, there are a number of subsections that refer to *techniques* of carrying out promotion. Most familiar on this list is advertising that uses the mass media. In this approach, efforts are devoted to reaching large numbers of persons with a single message. Provided that there is a great enough common interest among the receivers of the message, this form of advertising can be relatively efficient. The major difficulty is in creating a message that is meaningful to a substantial share of a given group of persons. Because this is hard to do, such advertising may often be wasteful and inefficient.

Another technique is one often referred to as *dealer promotion*. These efforts are primarily directed toward creation of selective demand—sale of a given brand. Such efforts cover a wide number of activities from window interior displays and demonstrations, to the use of premiums, combination offers, and free samples. The key to success for this form of promotion is voluntary cooperation and active participation of the retailer. The initiation of the effort, however, usually begins with the producer or manufacturer. The promotion may be a supplementary effort to enhance mass-media advertising, or the dealer program may stand alone as a separate form of promotion. In many situations, products, due to their lack of dramatic appeal, often cannot be advertised effectively, yet dealer promotion based on point-of-purchase materials may be just what is needed to give the product an extra boost in sales.

Consumer promotion is yet another technique in the promotional mix. Consumer promotional efforts are used to bring about rapid buying response on the part of the consumer by providing him with something "special" if he "acts *now!*" Because of the requirement of getting the consumer to act quickly, these methods are often referred to as *forcing methods*. All persons want to get maximum value for their money, so when a bargain or "something for nothing" is offered, the average person is strongly motivated to respond. The typical vehicles for such promotions are coupons, price-offs, combination offers, contests, and premiums.

In a recent study conducted by the Marketing Science Institute *Promotional Decisions Using Mathematical Models* (Boston, Massachusetts: Allyn and Bacon, Inc., 1967), some specific objectives for consumer promotions were mentioned:

1. Getting prospects to try a new product (forced sampling)
2. Calling attention to improvements in established products
3. Stopping the loss of old customers resulting from vigorous competition
4. Encouraging active point-of-purchase display and promotion
5. Helping and stimulating the firm's sales force

The use of consumer promotion is rather controversial. Critics claim that this approach is harmful because it centers attention on the promotional tool, rather than on the virtues of the product—that is, instead of emphasizing the product's good points, the consumer's interest is instead directed to the contest, premium, or other bargain that is available in the promotion. Basically, the firm ordering the advertising must decide whether the promotion will do a better job of getting the consumers to buy and use the product than mass-media advertising or other forms of promotion would.

One of the advantages of the consumer promotion approach relates to the consumer's ability to easily differentiate the product at either point-of-purchase or in use. If the product offers little brand discrimination in the eyes of the consumer, then the consumer promotion stimulus may be highly beneficial in creating additional sales and may even generate repeat purchases after the promotion is over. Another advantage is related to the publicity value of the promotion itself. The newsworthiness of the effort may generate much valuable editorial space that could not be gained through media advertising.

Although consumer promotions appear to have definite advantages to the user companies, there is much that these organizations need to understand and know to effectively use this technique. The Marketing Science Institute study previously referred to states the following:

It is plain that promotion plays an important role in marketing, but our knowledge of its effectiveness is lacking. The unfortunate facts that many promotional efforts seem to be prosaic, that no distinct goals are set, that post-audits are unimaginative, and that brand profits are jeopardized by intrinsic risks or wrong decisions may be attributed primarily from our inability to effectively tailor promotional endeavors to particular products, markets and circumstances. This problem of promotional selection is essentially the executive's responsibility, although effective research can assist in narrowing the areas for unaided judgement. [p. 17]

Thus, for any form of promotion, there are definite requirements of explicit goals, written objectives, evaluation of past performance, the use of experimental techniques to assist in decision making, and, finally, the need for well-planned and executed postaudits to determine the effectiveness of the promotional approaches.

Although a number of factors have been covered in the discussion of the balancing of the promotional mix, in the final analysis, a governing factor is the amount of money available for the promotional effort. Small or financially weak firms are likely to rely heavily on personal selling or dealer displays. Thus, businesses with large amounts of money available for promotion can make greater and more effective use of promotion than firms with limited resources. To illustrate more recent approaches in determining promotional strategy and planning a promotional campaign, the reader is referred to Appendix C, pages 213–16.

PROMOTIONAL FUNDING

To understand the financial aspect of the promotion mix, one should first consider promotional elasticity. Field, Douglas, and Tarpey, *Marketing Management* (Columbus, Ohio: Charles E. Merrill Books, Inc., 1966, p. 471), state:

Promotional elasticity measures the responsiveness of sales to changes in the amount of promotional effort, keeping the price constant. For example, if a 1.0 per cent increase in advertising will increase sales more than 1.0 per cent, then we can say that this product is promotion elastic; whereas, if sales increased by less than 1.0 per cent, then this good could be said to be promotion inelastic.

There are many factors which affect the promotional elasticity of a particular commodity. Some of the more important ones are: (a) the type of good in question (i.e., necessity vs. luxury), (b) the size of the promotional budget, (c) competition, (d) business conditions, (e) quantity of the product already sold, and (f) past expenditures for promotion.

None of these factors is easy to isolate or measure; however, in developing his promotional strategy program the marketing manager must try to take them into account. The concept of promotional elasticity is a very helpful analytical tool which can be useful in helping the marketing manager make better decisions.

It is further important to evaluate previous approaches to the financial decisions. Traditionally, patterns for the allocation of promotional budgets have generally been classed according to the following five practices:

1. Percent of sales: the forthcoming year's program is based on a fixed percent of sales for the year just completed. (At times the anticipated sales for the year ahead is used as the base.)

2. Fixed sum per unit: a dollar amount can be set per standard unit, either a unit of production or sometimes a packaged unit (a case).

3. Meeting competition: the method followed by many firms in industries where there is a successful and innovative firm which fills the role of being the industry leader. (It is geared to what works well or what the industry pattern seems to demand.)

4. Available funds: this is often the practice when the role of promotion is misunderstood or when funds are quite restricted.

Companies with a type of erratic growth may find finances must be allocated disproportionately to various areas as short-range needs have to be met. (At times a figure is picked on an arbitrary basis and this becomes a set amount.)

5. Task objective: the amount to be spent on promotion is determined by the type and amount of effort needed to accomplish specific marketing objectives or task objectives.

As the marketing concept becomes more fully recognized and accepted within industry, it is to be hoped that the last approach will become more common. But there is little actual evidence, outside of statements of some top corporate executives, that such is the case at present. Several years ago, in a study by Robinson and Luck, it was observed that there was little evidence of the scientific element in promotional decision making. The same statement could be made today. The key factor is immediate past performance. There is some relationship between this and present sales and project goals, but the most recent experience seems to be the principal guide.

The question then arises as to the greater knowledge that will be made possible through model testing and other scientifically oriented experiments. A potpourri of laboratory findings exists which suggest implications for the specialty advertising field. The peril, however, is that in many experiments dealing with human behavior, the laboratory findings bear little resemblance to reality. In the case of new hypotheses, the transition from artificial laboratory conditions in which limited variables are considered to the real world with a multitude of changing factors makes some of the findings appear meaningless.

Yet, progress is being made as reflected in a statement from the Marketing Science Institute study, *Promotional Decisions Using Mathematical Models* (Boston, Massachusetts: Allyn and Bacon, Inc., 1967, p. 23).

It would be as naive to suggest that it will ever be possible to inject a quantitative value for every factor into even the most elaborate model as to claim that the best answer can always be found through the employment of such models. Instead, the test is to see how many facets of the market can be blended into an adequate representation and whether a solution can be found better than those currently in hand. It no longer seems impossible, however, that adequate sets of definitional, behavioral, and institutional equations will be formulated with most of the pertinent elements included in a single model. We cannot afford to ignore the fact that analysis of complex marketing problems will be improved through the development of more complicated, more realistic models. There was a time when this was too costly, too time consuming, or just plain unfeasible. That time has passed for most practical applications in which large expenditures are at stake and for which suitable data can be obtained.

Each individual situation will determine the decision mix and should be approached as an opportunity to maximize results as related to objectives. Brink and Kelley in *Management of Promotion* (Englewood Cliffs, New Jersey: Prentice-Hall, Inc., 1963, p. 254) make this observation about advertising budgets:

> . . . there are no over-all rules for apportioning the advertising appropriation among the various media. Each market situation must be studied: and the ability of the various media available must be appraised to ascertain the best way to reach that market; then, the two are "married" to get the greatest coverage for the money. Some advertisers prefer to concentrate on one good medium and dominate it; others prefer a balanced choice to hit the prospects in as many ways as possible. Each system has its merits, but the majority of advertisers seem to favor the balanced medium choice.

Sell or advertise

It may be useful to summarize the points that relate to when certain forms of promotion should be used. Personal selling is most important under the following circumstances: (1) when the firm may have insufficient financial strength to carry out an adequate advertising program, (2) when the market is concentrated, (3) when the salesman himself is needed to establish rapport and create confidence, (4) when the product has a high unit value, (5) when demonstration is required, (6) when the product must be fitted to the customer's needs, or (7) when a trade-in is involved.

On the other hand, advertising becomes a major ingredient when the following conditions exist: (1) When the primary demand for the product tends to be increasing. (2) When there is considerable opportunity to differentiate the product from others that are available on the market. In effect, we are only saying that this condition provides the advertiser with something to say. (3) When the product has what might be termed "hidden properties." Thus the objective will be to inform and educate the public about these characteristics through the advertising. (4) Where powerful emotional buying motives exist for the product. Buying action is thus motivated through the stimulation of these motives. (5) Where the company has adequate funds to carry out such an advertising program. Thus, if a firm is in the position of meeting all or most of these conditions, then advertising may be the most effective promotional approach.

In utilizing any form of promotion, careful thought must be given to the effectiveness of the communication resulting from that application. There was a time when all promotion was conducted on a face-to-face basis. With this emphasis on the personal relationship, the message could be modified and corrected immediately in response to the attitudes of the prospect. The salesman, in effect, had a chance to feel out his prospect and explore his prospect's ideas and background. On this basis, he could then phrase his selling message in such a way that successful communication would result. If the message did not reach its mark, the salesman would realize this from the immediate and direct feedback he received from the customer and could then try again with a modified message. Under these circumstances, both parties were engaging in mutual role taking, and although there might still be communication difficulties, such problems were few compared to situations where mass media are used.

It would seem safest to concentrate marketing efforts in personal selling, were it not a necessity for many companies to carry out mass marketing. The need to reach large numbers of customers in a relatively short period and to motivate them to action has become paramount in our economic system. Although face-to-face communication still remains an important promotional method, most firms must utilize mass media approaches. Yet here one is faced with tremendous inflexibilities, because this mass market is made up of *individuals* who have different interests, values, and attitudes.

Market segmentation

Mass approaches to promotion must, therefore, attempt to break up or separate the members of a heterogeneous mass into more homogeneous groups so that more personalized messages may be beamed to them. This separation approach is better known as *segmentation analysis* and is the foundation of sound marketing strategy. In segmentation, one attempts to divide the total audience into relatively similar groups who have enough in common through shared social roles that communication can take place without direct role taking. To carry out this sort of division system, one must clearly define the market target and then study the background, attitudes, and interests of the population *before* advertising is carried out. Such effort is based on the supposition that in our economy each brand tends to sell effectively only to certain segments of any market and not to the market as a whole. In addition, marketing objectives must be based on knowledge of how segments that produce the most customers for certain brands differ in their requirements and acceptance of messages.

Groups or segments differ from others primarily on the basis of demographic characteristics. Therefore it would be useful to know facts about potential customers relating to their age, sex, occupation, income, education, size of family, and geography, just to name a few of the standard demographics. Though this information is relatively easy to obtain, some marketers believe that it is not likely to provide much direction for marketing strategy. Instead, they seek out the influences that motivate persons to buy or not to buy. For example, many marketing researchers utilize the *heavy-user* concept, meaning that the group of customers who use the greatest *quantity* of a given product are the most important group to influence. To take advantage of this concept, it is necessary to find the similarity of habits among these buyers and the most effective media by which to reach them and then to promote products on that basis. A businessman is thus doing nothing more than lining up the probabilities in his favor by promoting to those segments promising the highest potential communication and persuasion. Without segmentation, he faces the strong likelihood that much of the promotional effort will be wasted on the wrong people.

In applying segmentation analysis, one must remember that the market must be continually examined for critical differences in buyer motivations, attitudes, values, usage patterns, aesthetic preferences, or degree of susceptibility. The marketing manager who believes he already knows the best way of looking at a market is not doing his job. All ways of examining and segmenting that market must always be considered in order to choose those having the best possible implications for action.

Attention, of course, is centered on consumers' values, not absolute differences as reflected in the demographics. The same person who prefers a Cadillac automobile may shop for the cheapest brand of men's shirt. The person who spends thousands of dollars on a vacation trip may scrimp and save by buying only food items on special sale in the local supermarket. Such buyers have had different experiences within various product groups and thus retain different value-sets toward various products. The marketeering purpose is to identify those values and then promote products accordingly.

Segmentation analysis contributes a great deal more to an organization than simply dictating how its promotional dollars should be spent, however. It also assists greatly in designing a product line that will tend to fit the demands of the market, rather than fitting in some places well and in others very little or not at all; and it aids in providing early-warning information about trends in a swiftly changing market, thus allowing the company to take advantage of those changes.

In terms of promotion itself, segmentation analysis not only directs efforts toward certain groups in the market, it is also helpful in determining what appeals will be most effective for a promotional program. Possibly several appeals will be used, each to reach a different segment of the market. In following such a many-phased approach, an organization can attempt to quantify or forecast the segments of the market that will be responsive to each. Segmentation may also have a favorable effect on the timing of promotional efforts so that they occur at the time of year when selling resistance is at its lowest level and responsiveness is most likely to occur.

It is very likely, however, that even *within* homogeneous segments, there are certain persons who will be more easily influenced and reached by a particular promotion than others. The marketer must recognize that informal communication channels will complement the marketer-dominated channels. Marketers have for many years believed that one of the most effective means of communication is *word-of-mouth advertising*. That is, satisfied users can be of great assistance in furthering the cause of a given company's product. Product desire may, in fact, be best generated by observation of a product in the hands of another person. Seeing this, the potential buyer may then begin to make inquiries that will bring about his own greater awareness and initial interest. If this is the case, it would be highly useful to design advertising that will bring about an increase in informal communication and thus extend the mileage of promotional dollars. In this way the concept of opinion leadership also enters into the promotional process.

Opinion leadership simply means that within certain groups there are individuals whose behavior strongly influences other members of the group. The same persons are not the leaders or style setters for all activities and purchases; studies show that leaders and followers frequently change roles as areas of influence change. Leaders tend to be chosen on the basis of their knowledge and social position (what they know and who they know). An important characteristic of leaders, however, is that they tend to be more sensitive to mass media than do the followers in the group. As it applies to promotion, the informal channel is looked upon as being highly trustworthy— in effect suggesting that friends have no axe to grind. On the negative side, friends and neighbors may be looked upon by some members of the group as lacking in the competence necessary to provide detailed product information. Therefore, persons are moved to seek further information, and at this time advertisements and other promotional information may be sought. Thus, through promotion one may be able to stimulate and alter the flow of informal information in order to bring about maximum promotional benefit.

Efforts may, of course, be made to reach the opinion leaders directly. To do this, however, a method of identifying them is needed. Unfortunately, such a task is most difficult, especially in light of the changing roles mentioned earlier. The leaders may, however, demonstrate similar patterns of media exposure so that they can be reached with appeals tailored for them. Additionally, if marketers not only reach and motivate these opinion leaders to buy, but also enhance their satisfaction with their purchase, they will have moved significantly along the road to opening and using this information communication channel.

Specialty advertising can be especially useful in complementing the concept of market segmentation. The key to segmentation analysis lies in differences that exist between groups making up the general population. Once these groups are isolated, then each segment can be investigated separately with a view to finding the precise ad specialty item and message to appeal to that particular group. The major advantage that specialty advertising has over other media here is that it can be tailored to the specific group, no matter how large or (more to the point) how small the group happens to be. With mass media advertising, it is often impractical to address a message to a small segment and even more difficult to find a particular medium that will, without a tremendous amount of waste effort, effectively reach this segment. If there is any validity in McLuhan's concept of "the media (being) the massage (message)" then specialty advertising fulfills this task admirably.

Certainly in terms of the informal communications channels previously discussed, specialty advertising has an important edge over other media in many situations. The sight of a calendar or desk-top specialty item in the office of a respected person may be sufficient to influence social or business acquaintances in a favorable manner toward the advertiser. If a man displays or uses the specialty advertising material of a supplier, such display or use also demonstrates his confidence and favorable disposition toward the giver. Thus the medium can greatly enhance the word-of-mouth advertising approach which is so desirable yet so difficult to organize and manage.

A large part of the remainder of this book reveals how specialty advertising relates to the marketing and promotional mix, but a few prime observations can be made at this point. In the enhancement and implementation of the marketing concept, specialty advertising makes contributions in a number of important ways. First, it allows the firm to develop more adequately a close personal relationship with customers and prospects. By doing so, it assists in both creating and holding open a channel of communication between buyer and seller. The firm then has additional opportunity to contact and relate to its customers beyond simply promoting its services and products. Sending an ad specialty item leads to enhancement of the image of the company in the minds of the buying public, making it easier for the firm to research and explore the needs and wants of these members of the marketplace.

Cost considerations

Specialty advertising also makes a contribution to profit potential by making more precise the expenditure of promotional funds. Through careful choice of the persons to whom the ad specialties will be sent, a firm can allocate its promotional funds in a precise and specific manner, thereby more carefully incurring this important share of marketing expense. The direct result will be to bring about cost control for this important part of the marketing program, which, in turn, means greater profitability for the firm as a whole and more value to individual customers.

In the area of profitability, there is nothing on the business horizon which suggests that the trend of rising costs will change. "Controlled inflation" seems to be the future official federal economic philosophy. Among the largest classification of marketing costs are advertising and direct selling. Businessmen and researchers have for years tried to develop a fixed relationship between these two functions, but the variables are numerous, and the dynamic nature of the environment makes anything other than a general positive relationship just another hypothesis. Nevertheless, it is a safe assumption that as direct sales costs go up, more methods or approaches will be employed to increase efficiency. These will cover: increasing salesmen's potential productive time where they are actually communicating with a prospect or customer; increasing results of this time; reducing marginal accounts as they relate to direct costs of selling and servicing; reducing time spent on nonselling essentials (travel, parking, waiting for appointments, etc.); and effectively reaching people in purchase decision areas who are not normally seen in some direct sales efforts.

Creative cost control efforts will be employed in these areas on a consistent basis, even though there are factors that may offset improvements businessmen are able to make. As one observer stated: "With the right hand we increase marketing efficiency and with the other the system adds to the roadblocks of effectiveness." The use of specialty advertising cannot be recommended in all listed areas, but it is quite possible to use selected items to emphasize selling points, to reduce waiting time, or to reach more people who influence purchases.

Exceptions in marketing patterns

Although commonly accepted rules-of-thumb have been used in product policy, price policy, channel selection, logistics, and promotions as covered in this chapter, it would be wise to realize that noteworthy exceptions exist in successful marketing strategies. As will be discussed later, people buy want-satisfaction. If in meeting such needs a company uses a different, nontraditional approach that *works,* no rigid rule exists which states that the company is wrong. A company has its own capacities, limitations, or parameters within which it attempts to reach its objectives. If a company accomplishes this legally by using different tactics, then it has created its own success pattern. The dynamic nature of marketing and the growing complexity of the transaction process suggest that the exceptions to customary marketing approaches are likely to increase. One should keep in mind a few of the more well known, yet numerous examples: (1) Avon and Fuller-Brush selling convenience products door-to-door, (2) well-known local retailers (nonchain) selling to a national market (Marshall Field in Chicago and Neiman-Marcus in Dallas), (3) Sears Roebuck selling expensive art works and jewelry through catalogs, (4) expensive gourmet foods sold by mail, (5) a number of major oil companies selling consumer hard goods through their credit card system, and (6) services such as tax-assistance being offered by Sears Roebuck in their catalog offices and retail outlets.

Summary

By recalling the characteristics and advantages of the specialty advertising approach outlined in Chapter 1, it is not difficult to understand how well the medium assists in accomplishing the marketing requirements outlined in this chapter.

Differentiation of the product may be greatly enhanced through the use of the ad specialty item. First, the ad specialty can be designed to be a miniature version or illustration of the product itself, enabling the consumer or user to actually see the design features of the product. Second, the brand trademark may be designed into the ad specialty, allowing manufacturer or distributor differentiation to be more clearly supported and emphasized to the final user. Third, the very act of distribution of the ad specialty itself may help to distinguish the product or brand from others in the same product classification. Receipt of the ad specialty item may be sufficient to cause a product to have a psychological edge over those of its competitors! Fourth, the ad specialty may be designed to concentrate attention on only a particular characteristic of the product or service, thus enlarging and glorifying the primary trait that causes a single product to be different from all the others.

General merchandising application

THERE can be no doubt that the following statements about the strength and meaning of specialty advertising make the industry potentially one of the most significant growing forces in the promotional mix.

Specialty Advertising can help put advertising investment close to the point of becoming an economic science through the direction and control of circulation, the practical elimination of waste effor', and the injection of real personal appeal into the total advertising program.

. . . . .

Ideas are the main force of this sort of advertising; the specialty itself is a secondary matter. Think of Specialty Advertising as a motivating force in which ideas are the dynamo and specialties merely the cables of transmission.

Yet, these quotations were taken from Dr. Henry S. Bunting's book, *Specialty Advertising, The New Way to Build Business,* published in 1914 (Chicago: The Novelty News Press, pp. 1 and 37). What held the industry back? What kept it from becoming a more substantial force among all of the advertising approaches?

The problem of merchandising has been both the greatest challenge and, at the same time, a definite limiting factor for the industry.

As defined by the Committee on Definitions of the American Marketing Association, merchandising is "the planning and supervision involved in marketing the particular merchandise or service at the places, times, and prices and in the quantities which will best serve to realize the marketing objectives of the business." One of the major weaknesses that has affected the success of the specialty advertising industry is the somewhat random, even haphazard approach of marketing advertising specialties. This statement does not mean that *all* firms in the industry are deficient in this respect, but, in contrast to the success of some companies where salesmen average more than $250,000 per year sales volume, there are many other firms where salesmen average less than $50,000 volume per year. Additionally, the turnover of salesmen is dramatically high for the industry as a whole, and often a new man stays on the job for less than three months. These factors are the symptoms that point to the tremendous requirement facing the industry: *that of significantly improving the general merchandising methods used in marketing the industry's output.*

Industry structure

Another difficulty that has contributed to the merchandising problem has been the splintering effect of the industry's structure. Suppliers are in many cases highly production oriented. As mentioned earlier, their major function is to make products available to be sold through the distributors. In assuring themselves of profitable operations, these businesses see their personal interest lying primarily in the tight cost control of the goods they manufacture. Because of the imprinting requirements, it is usually not feasible or prudent for them to create and carry inventories of finished goods. Thus, they have sought and achieved a high degree of productive flexibility, allowing them to shift quickly in responding to the irregular demand received primarily through the distributors. Suppliers also find themselves only partially involved in the business processes that normally face a firm in the marketing of goods. Product development is one of their very important responsibilities, and yet these firms have only limited contact with the ultimate users of their products, making it difficult for them to understand consumer needs. Often their feedback is channeled almost entirely through the distributor, and forwarded in only a sketchy manner.

Communication between supplier and distributor is therefore a substantial part of the merchandising problem. This channel of communication is also constricted because of a weakness relating to the supplier's method of operation. There are certain instances where suppliers have chosen to sell directly to the advertiser, thereby cutting out or circumventing the position of the distributor in the channel of distribution. Although probably financially beneficial to the supplier, such action tends to undermine the effective business relationship that should exist between these two business types. Demoralized by this action, the distributor begins to reexamine his business obligations to the supplier, thus creating a situation where suspicion and distrust may color future dealings.

To further illustrate this industry structure problem, one must also look at the distributors' attitudes and operations. If the supplier is production oriented, the distributor is likely to be only sales oriented. In a classical, narrow sales-oriented tradition, the distributor frequently looks at his operation as one designed to sell the goods of his suppliers, rather than serving the needs of his business customers. Operating procedures and policies of the distributors are created to emphasize this point of view, and, as a result, two things happen. First, the businesses that are his customers and potential customers begin to think of the distributor's operation as being a peddling, gadget business. The distributor salesmen are then looked upon as being uncreative because they don't, viewed in this light, *appear* to be interested in the business problems of the customer. Instead, they seem entirely oriented toward selling products. Too often the salesman seems to be saying only, "I'm sure if you look through my catalog sheets we'll find something that will interest you in promoting your business!"

The second problem is tied directly with an earlier comment made about the supplier and is nothing more than an outgrowth of the sales-orientation problem. Because the distributor and his salesmen are so preoccupied with the problems of selling, they often fail to recognize or document the customers' needs which confront them and, therefore, cannot relay this information to the suppliers for their guidance in the creation of new products. Thus the supplier can only judge the adequacy of his products on the basis of the orders received for them. He is left with the typical research and development problem of having to guess what new products might be successful.

This communication problem creates another dilemma. Marketing, in the normal sense, must be a dynamic yet totally integrated process rather than one fragmented into functions or institutions. The specialty advertising industry structure makes it more difficult (though not impossible) to achieve this necessary integration. As a result, opportunities for synergistic effects may be lost, and even smooth working relationships are threatened. Instead of working as partners, the channel members may even look upon one another as competitors! To overcome this, industry elements must recognize that effective marketing is the result of the interaction of many activities, all of which must be carried out well for maximum success.

In order to dramatize this difficulty, let's look at the promotional effort devoted to advertising specialties. The supplier, because of his interest in products rather than needs, limits almost all of his promotional effort to three items: catalog sheets, samples, and advertising in the trade magazines. He thus directs his efforts toward reaching the distributor (through trade magazine advertising) and offering the distributor assistance in selling the supplier's merchandise. The distributor, on the other hand, with the exception of yellow-page listings and some (usually very little) direct mail work, places most or all of the remainder of his available funds in direct sales contact expense. Nobody, then, is promoting the medium to the general business community, except for the work done by the trade association.

Present budget practices

To get insight into current practices in methods used to budget specialty advertising, the authors contacted 50 large, well-known companies using this medium, followed by interviews with 50 small, single-owner business users. No attempt was made to establish these companies as a sample of a known universe. The main objective was to see if a pattern existed, based on one assumption: If some pattern evolved indicating how advertisers felt about the function of specialty advertising, this would be of value to the industry. The large companies contacted were quite diversified, representing consumer durables, industrial products, food, specialty and hobby products, and services. They were national in scope, with headquarter offices in every part of the country. The small concerns were primarily retail and service establishments located in and around Philadelphia, Pennsylvania.

The following general observations can be made according to the information received from the large companies:

1. Total advertising budgets were determined largely by a "summary of executive judgments," after which a question of "what can the company afford" was a major criterion. This is not to say that some of these judgments were without any scientific basis or made without consideration for marketing objectives. Proposals of advertising agencies were given heavy consideration, and many of these, even with admitted bias, have some element of research, analysis, and professional objectivity. In about half the companies, internal staff studies and proposals were used as they related to the companies' marketing goals. The principal executive in the budget formulation, as expected, was the advertising director, followed by the sales director. In a large number of these companies the president (as chief operating officer) was personally involved in this decision.

2. In those companies experiencing a downward pressure on profits or a reduced share of market, the archaic philosophy of "tighter financial control and reducing advertising budgets to conserve cash," still seemed to be of key importance. In spite of lip service to long-range outlooks and accepting the marketing concept, some large companies apparently still revert to a short-range, risk-control approach as financial goals are put under pressure. Opinions were volunteered, however, that this situation has improved somewhat over the past.

3. If the statement that total allocation of all advertising funds is subjective holds some truth, it holds even more when applied to the specific area of specialty advertising. Only two companies indicated that their advertising agencies planned the use of ad specialties as a part of the promotional mix. Generally speaking, most companies surveyed felt that their agencies were not interested in specialty advertising and considered the use of such items largely as being the companies' primary area of concern.

4. More than half the companies indicated that their manage-

ment classified ad specialties as a part of sales promotion as distinct from the advertising function. Comments used to describe specialty advertising were: "helps customer goodwill," "for out-of-town visitors to the company," "keeps the company image," "emphasizes some new product feature or service the company offers," "little 'thank you' items for customers' orders," "door-openers for our salesmen," "trade show traffic builders," "aids to highlight merchandise down the channels," "just good public relations," "helps in some employee relations," "used in plant openings."

5. Regarding other methods of "helping the company image" or "keeping customer goodwill," specialty advertising was considered significantly different, in comparison to customer entertainment, for example. A common theme was expressed that "entertainment is expected" whereas an ad specialty is a "little extra." Executive gifts were not thought of principally as advertising or promotion, but more as a "sales cost of doing business." In fact, most company executives mentioned that gifts came out of the sales department's budget.

6. Several companies using ad specialties at trade shows had in the past discontinued them, only to restore them subsequently. The original decision to drop them was entirely "to cut costs," and the decision to restore them was entirely due to "negative customer comments." One sales vice president said his company still had no basis to judge effectiveness of ad specialties, but "the overall reaction after we stopped giving away pens at our trade show was so bad we wouldn't dare drop them again." The thing that surprised him was that his company figured the cost per customer/prospect interview at the trade show (including cocktail parties, entertainment, accommodations, etc.) was slightly over $6. The cost per imprinted pen was 35¢. Yet the negative feedback about the absence of the pen was greater than the positive comments about all other activities in behalf of customers and prospects.

7. Some companies using ad specialties at trade shows felt repeated use of the same item gave them greater identity with that particular specialty, while others indicated they followed the practice of changing every year. No attempt had been made by any company to justify either policy. Sales management personnel indicated a greater awareness of what competitors used as ad specialties than they did of competitive mass media programs.

8. Although no executive being interviewed volunteered comments regarding relative differences in the effectiveness of methods

of distributing specialty items, they almost all agreed that distribution was very important. Experience was the principal guide in the method of distribution selected. Even after this decision was made, however, the actual techniques of the process of giving the item were likewise judged important.

In spite of these feelings, very few executives had ever brought up this subject in sales meetings or during sales training programs. Three company executives mentioned that this topic would hereafter be put on their meeting agenda.

The use of company sales personnel (except for items given to company visitors) was the primary method used to distribute specialty items. This further emphasizes that any instruction on "maximizing the effectiveness of distribution" that would be directed toward salesmen could prove to be important.

9. Very few executives of those companies contacted could recall an occasion where the specialty distributor salesmen provided ideas or demonstrated knowledge of the user companies' marketing problems. The main thrust was toward "what merchandise was available at what price." Some of the miscellaneous remarks which suggest an image of the industry's sales efforts are as follows: "Outside of the owners of these ad specialty businesses, their salesmen come and go like clockwork. They couldn't possibly get to know our problems." "They sell almost entirely from catalog sheets. If an item isn't on one of these sheets, they're at a loss as to what to suggest or to show us." "A few have suggested ad copy for the items we selected. But most of the time it's been a matter of 'what can't be done' in producing the message."

10. Many of the companies contacted did not sell through middlemen. But a few that did observed that *after* dealers were involved in sharing the cost of the specialties, they were more astute and discriminating in how and to whom the items were distributed.

The following general conclusions can be drawn from the information received from the small organizations which were contacted:

1. The decision on whether to use an ad specialty, and then which specialty, is primarily that of the head of the company. It is made in almost all instances after the supplier makes known what is available at what price. Consideration of what the specialty item is supposed to accomplish is usually given informally. In no case, however, was any research done relevant to these decisions. This observation, along with the others relating to small companies, is

not surprising, since the size of the company is very nearly the determining factor in the methods that are accepted and followed.

2. A major share or almost the total advertising budget is devoted to specialty items. Since it is, much more is expected of special advertising by the small companies. Almost all of the company owners considered this as advertising and not as sales promotion.

3. The principal comments used to describe specialty advertising were: "to attract prospects"; "to keep our name in customers' minds"; "to pass along information about our services, hours, phone numbers"; "to announce something new."

4. Relating the two previous observations, even though more of the men being interviewed in the small company classification felt specialty items were advertising, it can be said that they expected the merchandise being used to perform both sales promotion and selling functions.

5. Methods and techniques of distribution of items used are very important. (The respondents generally volunteered this comment.)

6. Comments about the representatives selling ad specialties indicated that salesmen showed a better feeling for merchandise suggested, but also revealed that they did not get to know the customers' businesses sufficiently. Salesmen turnover, emphasis on merchandise and price rather than ideas, problems of unkept delivery promises and short runs—were all mentioned several times. When a good sales approach was used (as was indicated by a few buyers), it stood out.

The general conclusion would be that intrinsically marketing executives do attach a value to the function of specialty advertising, but extrinsically their actions have not demonstrated that they can identify this value. It would seem that they would like to be shown some way to equate specialty advertising to their marketing needs and the available resources. It is obvious to many people involved in marketing that the role and function of promotion, and specialty advertising in particular, has not been adequately explored and explained. The user means well and feels that, "when we get the time, we'll go back and find out what happened." But the user also usually adds that he's not sure of how to find this out. Those in the industry who sell ad specialties as a group have not demonstrated sufficient ingenuity to have much acceptance by buyers. Their emphasis on merchandise and price is likely the greatest reason for this.

Users in small companies indicate a greater appreciation for and experience in the benefits of specialty advertising. But their expectations of its potential, of the best way to maximize results, and of its relation to total efforts and understanding of the receivers constitute a very real challenge for the industry.

To illustrate further the historic overattention given to price-approach selling in the industry, we quote the following editorial by Marvin Spike, appearing in the March 1970 issue of *The Counselor*. The ASI leadership (Advertising Specialty Institute, publishers of *The Counselor*) is certainly sensitive to the need for a more professional approach in the industry's direct selling efforts.

AN AUCTION OR AN INDUSTRY?

There he stood, hesitantly, (so the story goes), the daring, all-American hero-to-be. The nation's first astronaut held his breath for a moment, took one last longing look, paused and then finally entered his capsule. Days later, after successful completion of his mission, our hero was asked what kind of thoughts went through his mind during those last seconds before getting in and sealing the doors. His reply: "It suddenly dawned on me that I was entrusting my life and the mission to a mass of nuts, bolts and wires *designed and built by the lowest bidder.*"

Hopefully, in the case of America's space program, bid-contracts are awarded on something other than price alone and to date, with few exceptions, it's been successful. But even those exceptions have been tragic. They have cost lives.

Lives are not at stake in the buying and selling of ad specialties. But, the practice of "low-bid purchasing" results in the same doubts in the mind of the user and, all too often, results in too great a percentage of mishaps; exceptions that are costly to all concerned.

We're not taking a self-righteous stand for 100% list prices on every product, in any quantity, for every client, under any circumstance. That would be naive. Under certain circumstances, price has got to be *a* factor. But price does not always have to be *the* factor. Your client is entitled to be a careful buyer. But when price alone guides his purchasing, you owe it to him, to yourself and to the industry to prove that he's being careless, rather than careful.

Just what can you do? Plenty!

You can set minimum profit-percentage levels for yourself and for your salesmen, below which you refuse to accept an order. You can stay out of price wars and avoid the temptation to take any order at any price, just to keep an account or get a new one. When you find yourself up against a low-ball peddler, you can try to reason with your buyer, explain the doubts and problems . . . and if all else fails, step back and let him learn his lesson. He will, eventually. So will the peddler. It's economically impossible to sell *and service* without profit for any length of time.

If you're a supplier you can avoid quoting 101 distributors on substantial size orders. It's usually the big orders, requiring special quotes, that inspire price-cutting. So long as you have established policies, it's within your jurisdiction to avoid having the large orders footballed. Particularly on a repeat order, you can make it a policy to *protect* a distributor's right to a fair price by refusing to quote special prices or accept the business or utilize the cuts, artwork, molds or other essential materials for a specified period of time, except for orders placed by the distributor who originally sold that order.

As an industry, we can resist the temptation to put the pencil to the order pad at any price. If our pencil points are sufficiently competitive to start, not one of us needs to wear them down on profitless orders. Let's avoid having our industry's epitaph read *"designed and built by the lowest bidder."*

TWO ADDED STUDIES

The lack of stature among other advertising groups is another factor inhibiting the industry. In Chapter 2, we discussed the historical side of this same problem: the industry has never been fully accepted as a complete working partner in the promotional mix complex. In order to provide better insight into this difficulty, the industry has conducted two surveys that show a more positive acceptance than the studies just described. In a survey conducted among advertising agencies, about 45 percent said that they either bought or recommended ad specialty items for their clients. Additionally, more than 60 percent said that they themselves used ad specialty items to promote their own agencies among their clients. They added that because there is very little advertising directed to them by suppliers or distributors of the ad specialties industry, they rely almost entirely on ad specialty salesmen for information about specialty items.

In a second study conducted among advertising specialty distributors, additional insight was gathered concerning the barriers that distributors believe exist between advertising agencies and themselves. A sample of 223 distributors replied to a questionnaire regarding the business they do with various kinds of marketing agencies, including advertising agencies, sales promotion agencies, marketing consultants, and public relations agencies. It was learned that in the previous year, three out of four distributors called on advertising agencies, and one out of three had visited a public relations agency. More than 63 percent had reported sales to or through advertising agencies, with an average sales volume of almost $14,000 per agency. Only 23 percent reported sales to public relations agencies, with an average volume of almost $5,000 per agency.

In spite of this relative success, some startling facts were disclosed with respect to distributors' attitudes toward advertising agencies. Almost half of the ad specialty agency owners and managers agreed with the statement that, "Advertising agency personnel do not understand the specialty advertising medium and something should be done to 'educate' them." Still another 15 percent felt that the statement, "I have found that advertising agencies are not the least bit interested in specialty advertising items," was closest to their personal attitude. The respondents were also asked to write a statement that best described their views concerning advertising agencies. Of those statements, 84 were generally favorable, 72 were generally unfavorable, and the balance of 7 were unclassified. Typical of the "generally unfavorable" statements were the following:

"My relations with agencies are less than satisfactory. They *use* you, don't take you into their confidence, present a problem, and expect an answer the same day with delivery the next."

"I find that advertising agencies look to us for ideas and then go out and buy the items themselves."

"Ad agencies treat us as peddlers. They have the lowest echelon talk to us, steal samples and ideas, then try to buy directly. We avoid them if at all possible."

Among the "generally favorable" statements were:

"The agencies we work with have been excellent and appreciate our efforts to help them promote a product or an idea for their clients."

"We have worked with agencies for years on a small scale. We allow them a 15 percent commission or less on every sale that goes through them. Most of the time they ask us for suggestions for their advertising campaign."

"Advertising agencies can help us secure big volume on items with copy, especially those well designed, thus improving our image. They call me, then advise me of the program. I discover the vehicle. They do the art and copy."

It is obvious that there is a mixed opinion about the industry's relations with the advertising agencies, and much needs to be done to bring about a better understanding on both sides.

In addition to the barriers already described that prevent maximum merchandising effectiveness in the specialty advertising industry, the most basic and pervasive problem relates to the salesman himself. It has already been suggested that he used to be looked upon as a peddler rather than a counselor or problem solver. To some degree, this problem continues to exist throughout the industry, although the Specialty Advertising Association International (SAAI), has attempted to solve this problem. The solution will follow three major paths: selection difficulties, the training function, and creating a challenge that will provide the motivation necessary to retain good personnel.

Building the sales force

In selecting salesmen, the industry faces competition from almost all other forms of selling activity. Because of past reputation, a specialty advertising selling job is often looked upon as being less desirable than other selling positions. For this reason, many who are interested in applying tend to be persons who have failed to find opportunities in more prestigious industries. Because of this, the recruiting effort must be very carefully handled so that effective screening can be carried out. In order to follow through with proper training and supervision, the organizations in the industry *must* select persons who are indeed trainable.

Recruiting, then, becomes a critical aspect in the selection process. This effort can utilize newspaper advertising, personnel agencies, contacts with other businessmen, and referrals by a company's own salesmen and by sales personnel employed by other companies. Depending on the needs of a particular firm, these sources can be followed continuously or used only as vacancies arise. The general practice of the industry is the assignment of territories on a nonexclusive basis. Therefore, up to some practical limit, new territories can be created relatively easily.

Another vital part of the selection task is to evaluate properly the applicant's strengths and weaknesses and the potential problems that the company and the salesman may be facing together. A primary part of this task involves the interview of the applicant, which must accomplish two things. First, the interview is designed to provide a first-hand evaluation-impression of the person being interviewed. Second, the interview provides the interviewer the chance to sell the applicant on the merits of the opportunity. Unfortunately, many recruiters have made the mistake in the past of overselling the benefits and challenges of a position. To aid in the development of these necessary interviewing skills, a part of the Executive Development Seminar, held annually by SAAI, is devoted to this important subject.

The final step involves the actual hiring, which is the real decision-making part of the task of selection. Such standard activities as receiving a complete application form or resume, evaluating it and checking previous employment, references, and credit must become regular steps in the hiring process. The applicant's materials must be thoroughly and objectively evaluated before a decision can be made as to whether a man will be worth the time and money spent on his training. The quality of the men selected will largely depend on the intensiveness of the recruiting effort and the skill, objectivity, and judgment of the recruiter.

As previously suggested, some persons who seek employment in the specialty advertising industry often do so on a second choice basis. Yet, as a whole, the industry has thrived on the basis of finding individuals who "try harder" to demonstrate that they can indeed become effective sales personnel. The fact that the industry may have provided another chance for persons who have not found success elsewhere could be viewed as a strength of this field and a factor for which it should be commended.

TRAINING—GENERAL

SAAI has instituted a number of programs to assist members in carrying out the training task. At the salesman's level, the association has created a series of training booklets which can be used either for self-development or utilized in a formally conducted program. These basic materials cover fundamental sales techniques as well as specific approaches that have been found to be effective by other ad specialty salesmen.

The initial starting point required for the successful salesman in specialty advertising is to have a basic knowledge of the medium. The representative must know what kinds of things can be accomplished through the use of advertising specialties. For example, one of the most important applications of the ad specialty item is to help a business become known, that is, convey the image of the company to persons who don't know that it exists. This is always a problem facing a new firm, and even more established organizations must reach new potential customers.

The second basic accomplishment is to attract and hold customers. Although an organization may have had the opportunity to serve particular businesses in the past, such previous sales are no guarantee that they will be receiving new business from those same organizations in the future. Through the use of ad specialties, businesses can effectively keep their name before potential customers by a "special" means, in addition to the use of catalogs and brochures.

A third basic element is that ad specialties can be used effectively to say "thank you" and "please." In other words, they can project gratitude for past business and can further be tailored to ask for additional business. Often a company and its salesmen find it both awkward and difficult to say, "May we please have your future business?" Ad specialties can serve to convey this message easily and comfortably.

Certainly ad specialties can also serve the highly important public relations function of communication with the public in order to secure its understanding and goodwill. Therefore, the motto or slogan in or on the ad specialty can convey the philosophy, policy, and practices of a firm. The General Electric slogan, "Progress Is Our Most Important Product," can be, and frequently is, used on many different items. "You can be sure if it's Westinghouse" is an equally successful competition message. Specific ad specialties have been chosen because they convey the image of "progress" as a result of their unusual design or other advantageous qualities.

TRAINING—SPECIFIC

One of the larger companies in the specialty advertising industry takes an interesting approach in training salesmen on how to recognize the uses of advertising specialties. The system categorizes the reasons for buying in terms of eight basic sales. Some of the categories are general, potentially applicable for almost any of the 10,000 ad specialty products, while others are specifically oriented toward certain ad specialty items.

In the "specific" area, there are three that are essentially calendar advertising sales. These include, first, the *indoor billboard* sale, which is in effect a large (the larger the better) calendar hanging in a public place. An illustration of such a calendar is the one distributed by Pan American Airways each year. Because of the high quality of artwork, the general attractiveness, and the tastefulness of this calendar, it is displayed in many businesses and public buildings, thereby providing the company with a very high level of exposure to their promotional material.

The second sale is the *home calendar,* where the advertiser's name is displayed on the walls in homes of people he is trying to reach. Often these displays are so desirable that the recipient will frequently thank the giver for the opportunity to display the calendar in the home. The third category, closely related to the home calendar, is the *business office calendar,* which serves essentially the same purpose as the home calendar.

The *pocket business card* sale, another specialty advertising category, can take an unlimited number of forms, such as a pocket calendar, a writing instrument, or a key case. The idea is quite simple: Take the information found on the typical business card and somehow place it in the prospect's or customer's pocket. Chances are, the pocket business card will remain in the customer's pocket because it is desirable and useful. What item is used is not so important as long as it has particular personal value so that the customer is likely to carry the object with him.

Another sale which logically follows the pocket business card, is the *desk business card.* The intention here is to present something novel or special enough to induce the customer to want to display the product on his desk. Items include desk calendars, ash trays, rulers, shears, trays, holders, and many other ornamental as well as useful articles.

The sixth sale is termed *customer insurance,* which implies that the advertising companies are really not interested in giving things away. Rather, they have a very important objective in mind when they send ad specialties: They are interested in insuring good customers, who were won at great cost and effort, against loss to competition. The underlying assumption is that indifference is the primary factor causing a company to lose a customer. The customer insurance approach aids the businessman in making certain his customer will remember that his business is appreciated and not taken for granted—really nothing more than good customer relations. The ad specialty is not intended to take the place of a cocktail, a game of golf, a lunch, or a dinner, but it does an outstanding job of supplementing that kind of personal customer relations effort.

Another form of sale, the seventh, is through *direct mail*. Here we are not discussing direct mail in its normal advertising sense but in terms of the ad specialty devices that may be conveyed conveniently and easily through the mail. The typical businessman is not always in a position to be handed a gift, so direct mail is often used as a device to remind him of a company's interest in him. Thus, the direct mail piece may only take the form of a notice that the advertiser's business still exists and that he values the continued relationship. He may do this in either a light-hearted or serious manner. Frequently the firm is not working for long-term effect but is interested in a brief, yet memorable, reminder.

Finally, we have the *business greeting* sale, which might properly be considered a long distance handshake. Often, new prospects are reached through this approach. It is a way of telling prospective customers that the business exists and is willing and ready to serve the customer's needs. This is perhaps the simplest and easiest of the sales to understand and needs no amplification here.

These eight sales (or reasons) for specialty advertising are not exhaustive. There are, of course, many more logical and necessary applications of ad specialty use, but the eight categories do simplify teaching the new salesman the basic types of utility for the items.

SELLING TECHNIQUES

Before ever starting the sale, however, the salesman must be sensitive to the basic elements of prospecting, routing, and planning. In the prospecting phase of preparation, the salesman should consider the types of prospects he is seeking. At the minimum, he must seek those businesses that can, in fact, buy what he is selling (thus eliminating such organizations as schools, government offices, and others that are illogical prospects for ad specialties). The salesman must also be sure that the distributor will be paid for the goods sold to the customer. The salesman is expected, therefore, to avoid organizations likely to be poor credit risks. Finally, the salesman must seek those companies that will order items that can profitably pay the salesman for the time he invests in serving the account.

Typically, the salesman either uses an area plan of canvassing, calling on all businesses in a given region, or he canvasses similar businesses in a wider given area, such as banks or restaurants. He should also follow the newspapers closely to find out about new businesses opening in the area that may qualify as new accounts. This prospecting phase may be one of the most important for the salesman and should be carried out thoroughly and correctly.

Planning the selling effort for specialty advertising is not too dissimilar to that used in most other forms of personal selling. Basically, the old "plan your work—work your plan" adage applies equally well to this form of salesmanship. The "who-what-why" approach for the ad specialty salesman includes the following considerations:

1. The salesman should be prepared to talk to the prospect about a specific promotional problem. It should be something that the salesman has carefully thought through in terms of the prospect's potential needs. Almost any business has at least the needs of (a) getting more new customers and/or (b) doing more volume with the business' present customers.

2. Included in the salesman's problem solution should be recommendations for distributing items to the customers and to prospects.

3. Where appropriate, the salesman should also propose certain advertising copy that will help make the ad specialty effective and give it more impact.

Industry assistance.   All of these considerations tend to imply a knowledge of each kind of business upon which the salesman is calling. The background necessary to do this job can, of course, come with experience. As the man calls on different kinds of businesses, he develops an insight into both common and specific problems of those businesses. For the new salesman, SAAI publishes a series of brochures called *The Facts of Business.* Each two-page booklet offers a summary of facts relating to a particular industry, along with a representative list of problems and solutions that are common for that particular industry.

An example of *The Facts of Business* folders is one devoted to the photographic industry. The typical business operations in this industry are listed, including photographers, photo finishers and processors, retail and wholesale camera stores, and equipment manufacturers. Additionally, statistics are provided relating to the number of units of each type as enumerated in the *Census of Business,* along with the estimated annual sales volume of each. Then, information is provided that briefly describes typical problems that businesses in this industry face. As an example:

Today's professional photographer is often comparable, in talent and temperament, to the artist. Those most successful in portraiture specialize in photographing business leaders and socially prominent people.

Key Point—A receptionist scans the daily paper for names of prominent people who have been appointed directors, officers of a company, an association, or financial institution. A letter of congratulations together with a lasting advertising gift is sent.

Key Point—As this man continues to climb his ladder of success, he begins to receive more and more requests for his picture for news releases. Mail advertising specialties to remind him that his features are constantly changing and the years have slipped by since his last photos were taken.

Finally a few common advertising slogans that pertain to that industry are included to give the salesman ideas for suggesting specific phrases to be imprinted on the ad specialty.

Similar information folders are available for other industries, such as restaurants, motels and hotels, milk dealers, funeral directors, drug stores, and many others. Thus, the salesman receives much assistance in carrying out his planning efforts.

The advertising specialty salesman, confronted with the same problem that almost anyone in customer contact work faces, has only a very few moments in which to create interest on the part of his prospect. Some experts claim that the typical salesman has only 20 seconds to bring about this attention and interest. As a result, he must act quickly in order to get his point across. The attention of prospects is seldom ready-made, but must be obtained in perhaps the first ten words the salesman says. Although the prospect may have a need for advertising specialties, seldom does he have a predisposition to buy something. Instead, he is usually thinking, "What

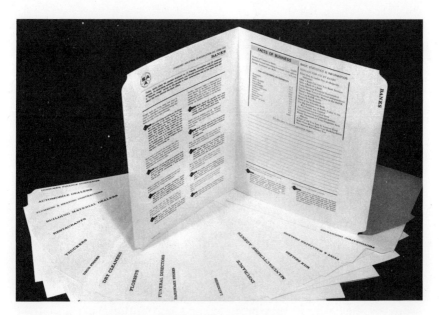

The association's *Facts of Business* brochure selection.

SAAI "How to" sales aids folders for sales personnel.

can this product do for me?" The essence of the effort is that the salesman is really selling new customers, sales stimulation, or customer loyalty, rather than an ad specialty item.

The key to this form of creative selling is to arouse purchasing desire in the customer. The prospect will then *want* to buy the protional program. In order to do this, the salesman must find out what the main advertising or marketing problem of the prospect is, tell the prospect how the program can help to solve it, and excite the prospect about how pleased he will be to see the item actually accomplishing the job. In the final analysis, the real clincher is the problem-solving capacity of the ad specialty item itself. It is presented to the prospect only after the salesman has explained how appropriate it will be in accomplishing the objective created for it. If the salesman has made the prospect enthusiastic about the ability of the ad specialty item to help him, he can present higher-priced items. If he conveys the attitude that he is excited and enthusiastic about the item, the prospect will catch some of this and his interest will grow in like manner. In a sense, the moment of presentation of the item is the opportunity for the salesman to demonstrate his ability at showmanship and dramatization to build up the impact of the product.

Sales resistance.   In any form of sales work, it is common to run into situations where the prospect raises objections. Actually, by doing this, the prospect is indicating that his interest is aroused, but that he is psychologically resisting. The prospect may say that he "doesn't need any," and in many cases he actually means it! Often, however, he is simply looking for more reasons in order to justify the decision that he is trying to make. Second, he may be just stalling in order to make conversation or to test or match wits with the salesman. Third, the salesman may well have simply failed to make himself clear during his presentation. He may not have told the complete story that reflects the need for the advertising specialty. Total presentation includes explaining that the need can be satisfied by placing the order, that what the salesman is suggesting is best for the potential customer, that the salesman and his company are the ones that the prospect wants to do business with, and, finally, that *now* is the time to buy! If any of these facets has not been covered by the salesman, objections are almost sure to be brought up.

Skill at handling objections is critical, especially to the advertis-

ing specialties salesman, for frequently the benefits that the salesman is selling in this business seem quite intangible, at least for
the moment. For this reason, the salesman has to be very adept in the
techniques for handling objections. There is a standard, six-step procedure that is advocated by many in the industry. It begins with the
salesman first expressing understanding of the prospect's objection.
This must be done in a positive way, so it does not appear that the
prospect was stupid or naïve in making the objection in the first
place. After having expressed this understanding, the salesman must
then quickly qualify the kind of objection that was raised. Third,
after having decided what caused the prospect to bring up this point,
the salesman restates the objection. Fourth, after making sure that
both the salesman and the prospect clearly understand the objection, the salesman answers it. He might do this using any of the following forms:

1. "Yes—but"—Admitting the soundness of the position, the
salesman indirectly denies that the objection is a valid one.

2. Compensation—Having admitted the validity of the objection, the salesman goes on to make additional points that tend to
minimize the objection.

3. Ask a question—In order to get the prospect to talk, the
salesman may ask for more information about the objection. In effect, he is saying, "Why do you feel that way?"

4. Turn-about—The salesman actually changes the objection
into a reason for buying!

5. Direct denial—Under some circumstances, the salesman must
directly indicate that he believes that the objection is clearly invalid.

Fifth, after having answered the objection, the salesman asks the
prospect if he has answered it. If so, he proceeds with his sales story.
An objection must be handled immediately or the prospect may hear
nothing more (figuratively) until his objection *is* answered.

DISTRIBUTION PLAN

Other advertising media have their own built-in distribution plans.
Magazine, newspaper, and TV advertisements are all carried directly
to the public without any distribution efforts on the part of the advertiser. The advertiser using ad specialties, however, must also
distribute the item which carries his advertising message. Because

he has probably had little skill or experience in such distribution, he tends to rely heavily on the judgment of the ad specialties salesman for advice and help. There is no question that the distribution plan may be the critical key to the successful use of an advertising specialty. Thus, for the good of the salesman in making future sales, it is imperative that he give proper time and attention to this phase of the sale. Traditionally, this has been one of the weakest parts of sales in the industry.

Basically, there are only three standard forms of physical distribution for advertising specialties. The first is personal distribution by the businessman or his employees when customers and prospects come to the advertiser's place of business. The prospect or customer may simply enter the business establishment in the normal course of patronizing it, or may be responding to a direct mail invitation to come in and "Pick up the free gift reserved for you." Although there may be many reasons for using this plan, it basically benefits the business by actually getting people on the premises. (Some of the applications of this plan will be described briefly later in the chapter.)

The second basic method of physical distribution is to go directly to the homes or places of business of customers and prospects. This method is particularly useful because it demonstrates to the recipient that the advertiser is going out of his way to do something nice for him. The advertiser is thus making a special effort to reach prospects and customers, and this is usually noticed and appreciated. Certainly this technique would be looked upon as more soft sell than when the ad specialty is distributed in the place of business.

The third approach is to distribute the ad specialty by mail. Although for the most part less expensive and time consuming for the advertiser, this method is also looked upon as far less personal than either of the first two approaches. The mail method is highly flexible, however, and potentially reaches far more people than either of the others. The "in-store" method requires the recipient to enter the business establishment, which he may not feel a strong motivation to do. The "non-store" presentation method is limited by the sheer volume of stops that have to be made, often over a wide geographic area. Both of these techniques may reach the prospect or customer at an inconvenient time, perhaps causing impatience or irritation. But the mail approach is much more geared to the convenience of the recipient.

In addition to physical distribution, however, there is also a *timeliness* dimension that is critical with respect to distribution of advertising specialty items. Not only must the advertiser decide how he will physically distribute the items, but he must also decide *when* he will give them to the recipients. This time consideration can be broken down into two categories: time concentration distribution and special event distribution.

Time concentration distribution is used when large groups of recipients are to be reached at a single point in time, say the distribution of executive gifts or ad specialties at Christmas. Typically, distribution for this occasion is concentrated in the two or three weeks preceding the holiday. Used to create goodwill and to say "thank you," the Christmas plan can utilize each of the three distribution methods previously discussed.

The store traffic plan is another illustration of time concentration distribution. Generally, the retailer or businessman mails or distributes a postcard folder or handbill which offers a free gift to those who will come to the store and get it. Often such a plan is accompanied by some additional reason for coming to the store, such as a new building, new season, or new line. Usually, an end-of-free-offer deadline is included to speed response. Still another variation of the time concentration distribution category is the customer registration plan, where store customers are asked to register for their free gift. Later, when the ad specialty arrives, the recipients are asked to stop in for the item. Thus, the business has two opportunities to get people into the shop, and, additionally, they have been able to accumulate an excellent mailing list. Because the customer has asked for the gift, there is little question that he will appreciate and use it.

Special event distribution, on the other hand, is used to recognize that something has been fulfilled or accomplished that should be honored with the award of an ad specialty product. Generally, there is no prior commitment by the advertiser in making this presentation. Instead, it occurs because of its impact value. The end-of-payment plan is a form of such an event. Often, goods are financed by consumers, and what better time is there for the businessman to

attempt to get additional business from an old customer than at the
end of the payment period? It is at this time that the customer may
have new money to spend. But the special event distribution may also
occur at the beginning of a business relationship, rather than near
the end. The thank-you-for-the-order plan specifically acts to
demonstrate to this new customer that the firm is pleased to include
"him" or "her" among its clientele. They are therefore happy to send
a gift as a "thank you" for the confidence the customer has shown
in them.

Two other forms that fall under this heading are the birthday and
anniversary plans. Some firms, such as insurance companies, already have birthdates or anniversary information on file, but others
would have to ask for the dates. A variation on this is the "birthday"
of a particular purchase, such as three years since the customers
bought the car they are driving. Each of these plans brings special
attention to a particular happening that is of importance to the customer or prospect, so the receipt of the ad specialty is likely to have
a good effect on the customer.

COPY RECOMMENDATIONS

The salesman must consider four basic premises before attempting to write or recommend advertising copy for the specialty. First,
he must consider *what the item is supposed to do*. If the ad specialty
is used to emphasize the date of a convention or anniversary of a
business, say, the copy is then the reason that the specialty item is
bought, and therefore the item must enhance the date and give it
added impact. If the specialty is used to announce a new product
or model, then the copy would be written to do this job more effectively.

The second consideration is *who gets the item*. A different type of
message would be addressed to children than to adults, to sports car
enthusiasts than to family car owners, and so forth. A given businessman may be trying to reach more than one group of people. As an
example, a savings and loan association may be trying to reach
homeowners and potential homeowners on the one hand and, on the
other, may want to direct a message to real estate brokers and
builders.

Third, *the item itself* can have an important effect on what copy is written. Sometimes the ad specialty can itself be directly connected with the business, such as a pen shaped like a bowling pin used at a bowling alley. There are other items that, by their very nature, suggest a copy theme. Typical of these are coin banks with the copy, "You can bank on our services," for example, or rulers that say, "Make it a rule to shop at . . . ." It should be noted that the item itself may suggest that copy be omitted. In most cases, it would be inappropriate to imprint an advertising message on an expensive executive gift such as a leather briefcase or a desk clock.

The fourth consideration is *the space available* on the item itself. When the copy is of prime consideration and the advertiser has a lot to say, the item must often be selected so that it can accommodate the message. In other cases where the item is the key to the sale, the copy must conform to the space available to it.

The writing of the copy is done within the context of good writing procedure, but brevity is especially important when writing copy for ad specialty items. While brief, the copy must also suggest customer benefits. It thus should relate to why the prospect or customer should do business with the advertiser. The benefits may be either implied or stated. Examples of a stated benefit would be "Atlantic keeps your car on the go." The implied benefit may be something like "Founded in 1902," implying that a firm that has been in business 70 years must be dependable and reliable; or, "Ours is a business that service made," implying that the prospect can also expect good service with his purchase. Additionally, the copy may be a question-answer form, such as "Low price? You bet!"; or utilize a rhyme such as "Made stronger—lasts longer." Finally, the copy may take the form of a slogan that will be repeated over and over.

The final consideration with respect to copy writing is the layout. Copy should be arranged so that it attracts attention, makes reading easy, and puts the advertising message across. Usually the layout will lead off with the message, followed by the company's name. Because the "why" is the advertising message, it should take priority over the firm's name, though both may be equal in type size.

All of these factors relate to improving the merchandising approach of the average salesman, making him something more than just a peddler. In a sense, the advertising specialty salesman can become a counselor. He can acquire and accumulate skills that will allow him to become a professional member of the marketing team.

No longer is he necessarily just a salesman making available a wide range of products to be used in promoting a business. He can become a problem solver for his business customers. We are not suggesting that the salesman always functions in this skilled way; often he is prevented from doing so by clients who are either unwilling to use his talents in this way or unaware that he can perform advisory roles.

Association involvement

SAAI has further contributed to professionalization with its annual Executive Development Seminar, first held in conjunction with Case Western Reserve University of Cleveland, Ohio, and subsequently moved to the University of Missouri at Kansas City. A very intensive eight-day (and night) program covers a variety of subjects, including discussions on the industry's image, marketing systems, promotional mix, marketing techniques applied to advertising specialties, accounting procedures, employee interviewing, selection and motivation, employee training, and communications techniques, both written and oral. Like other seminars, however, much of the real value for the participants arises out of the interaction and exchange of ideas among the individuals in attendance. These seminars were initiated in 1961 and have since served over 300 members of the industry. Although this number appears small, the effect on the industry has been far-reaching. Enrollment is limited to 35, and each year many interested people are turned away because of lack of available space. Those who have attended look upon the designation "Certified Advertising Specialist" (C.A.S.), which they receive upon successful completion, as of special significance. The graduates have generally worked hard to incorporate their training into the operations of their businesses. A postgraduate seminar has also been instituted in recognition of the need for continued development.

To supplement the Executive Development Seminars, which are aimed at training management personnel, SAAI has developed a Sales Clinic program that is designed to reach the typical ad specialty salesman. Clinics have been held on a regional basis across the country, serving hundreds of salesmen. The Sales Clinic is established on a very operational basis, utilizing a diagnostic approach to

SPECIALTY ADVERTISING ASSOCIATION

In recognition of satisfactory completion of the

SAA Executive Development Seminar

conducted at University of Missouri at Kansas City

William R. Williams

is officially designated to be a

CERTIFIED ADVERTISING SPECIALIST

and is granted the privilege of wearing the C.A.S. emblem

and of using it in his business activities.

1971

PRESIDENT   CHAIRMAN, Education Committee

The official C.A.S. plaque for Executive Development Seminar competition.

consulting. The salesman is urged to use certain probing questions in order to pinpoint the objective of the firm he is trying to serve. He then delves into a series of factors that are needed in preparing to accomplish the objective. Typical of the sales training objectives are the discussion of techniques to accomplish the following: (1) to isolate groups—what, where, and who are the prospects? (market segmentation); (2) to determine where the buying decision is made; (3) to determine the advantages of the company's products or services; (4) to determine what the goal is worth to the client; (5) to discover what has been done previously; and (6) to agree on a specific target. If the salesman properly identifies all of these points, he will have sufficient insight into the business's needs so that he can proceed to prescribe a program. The clinic involves role playing and participation, with much effort devoted to demonstrating the efficiency of the approach and bringing about confidence in its use.

Behavioral sciences

I F members of the ad specialties industry can develop deeper insight into the nature of behavior patterns of the users (the ultimate receivers of specialty items as apart from their purchasers), then the place of this advertising medium in the promotional mix is bound to be enhanced. At the end of this chapter, ten of the most commonly asked questions regarding the relationship of behavioral science and the use of ad specialties are posed, together with their answers. No one disciplinary approach can be emphasized, since the ultimate buying decision, the consumer behavior analysis, and anything else needed to understand the why behind our human activities must draw information from many areas. Essentially, concepts must be studied and related on an interdisciplinary basis. One must therefore turn to those groups of scientists that have historically been concerned with gathering data on human behavior. Among these groups are the social and cultural anthropologists who have studied different ways that cultural patterns have developed and various means by which groups have solved living and communications problems. General, motivational, social, and clinical psychologists have developed improved understanding and insight into individual behavior, along with the sociologists who emphasize group influences and relationships.

People are, in fact, dynamic, complex creatures. In spite of the simplicity of the act of giving an individual a book of matches or a ball-point pen, the recipient remains an individual. As mentioned by Engel, Wales, and Warshaw in *Promotional Strategy* (Home-wood, Illinois: Richard D. Irwin, Inc., 1967, p. 53):

It cannot be stressed too heavily that successful promotion must be oriented in terms of and not against basic buyer predispositions and motive states. It is necessary to reject a philosophy which assumes naively that one persuasive message invariably is appropriate for all. Selective promotion recognizes clear-cut individual differences, and the promotional program is designed with these variations in mind.

We can turn this statement around for the moment to point out the same inherent complexity in the human variables of the giver. Selective perception (discussed in greater detail below) can also be a factor here. A member of the industry who feels his job ends with the sale of the merchandise may well be successful on a financial basis for the short term. He may consciously refuse to use the larger challenge of the role of the industry. Yet the study of buying patterns must take into account that the buyer is often not the consumer or user. From a marketing standpoint, this must be emphasized and repeated. The buyer is likely to be influenced by the user, but there are also other reference groups or individuals with a strong voice in the purchase decision. Accordingly, strategy designed to bring about the purchase of a certain good or brand should involve all of the influencing units that can be reached through various types of communications.

Examples are abundant. A food product for babies is a simple illustration. The mother would normally be the buyer, the child the consumer, and in varying degrees of influence, other parties who might sway the purchase could include a pediatrician, a friend, neighbor, grandparent, an older brother or sister—even a newspaper columnist. The marketing message naturally can't reach them all in the same way, so by careful analysis and a priority assignment, the promotional effort is directed toward the most important groups.

Thus, for the benefits of all parties involved in marketing efforts, and to fill the increasing need for true advertising counseling, the total spectrum of reactions of all who come in contact with an ad message should be considered. This is no easy task. Nevertheless, the ability and willingness to study and view certain items as others do is the only basis for progress and growth for any industry. For specialty advertising this may well mean that a situation develops in which some successful merchandise items reach saturation points, or diminishing acceptance makes it advisable to drop popular items. Current efforts to downgrade cigarette consumption could create a problem for any firm that remains associated in any way with making it easy or popular to smoke. This is just a hypothetical example, but if it is valid, it could affect the use of matches as a promotional item. Even more important, methods of distribution of ad specialties may prove to have far more psychic return for the receiver than the value of the item itself.

As in all fields associated with promotion, the goal of the efforts and funds expended is to influence buying behavior. This means human behavior. In spite of the feeling that the reasons for much of what people do is to a large degree not known to them, behavior does have a theme of organized relationships underlying it. Responses and reactions are all related to an individual's perception. This perception—his picture of the moment—is a summary of his value system, experiences, needs, education and training, physical attributes, environment, cultural and religious background, and mental set. Tillman and Kirkpatrick in *Promotion—Persuasive*

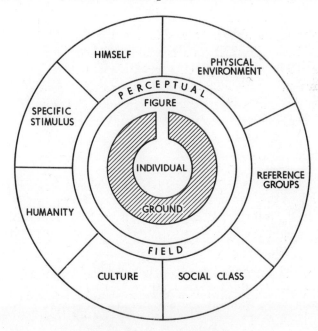

An individual's perceptual field.

Communication in Marketing (Homewood, Illinois: Richard D. Irwin, Inc., 1968, pp. 73–74) explain the *perceptual field* with a diagram representing seven dimensions which contribute to individual behavior. They state that "much of the perceptual field is contained in ground—the past perceptions and differentiations of the individual, which both result from his perception and influence the perceiving process." The seven dimensions "are not exclusive. They interact with one another to make the perceptual process even more complex." Also, as each person can attest, there is sometimes conflict in these categories mentioned. This causes even greater complexity in understanding human behavior.

This overview is valuable, but it is important to analyze the "Himself" segment even further. One of the chief benefits from recent steps in studying and understanding the processes of buying and consuming is the demonstrated need to study *systems behavior* or overall relationships of all human activities. We should equate total behavior, avoiding any conclusion that acts of people are isolated and unrelated. Doing this, however, creates conflicts with the sacred premises of specialists who tend to concentrate on single approaches in analysis.

In spite of the interlocking and binding relationships of many factors, ten will be individually examined. These are felt to be the most pertinent to the specialty advertising field. By alphabetical order they are: (1) adoption, (2) association, (3) attention, (4) emotion, (5) learning/memory/retention, (6) motivation, (7) needs, (8) perception selection, (9) reward, (10) set.

ADOPTION

The concept of adoption involves the various steps that an individual goes through in the acceptance or rejection of a product or service. In the following description, it is probable that specialty advertising would relate more to the "awareness" and "trial" stages. This flow process, of course, changes, depending on the novelty appeal of the product, the price, the technical aspects, and other major factors. (From Steven J. Shaw, "Behavioral Science Offers Fresh Insights on New Product Acceptance," *Journal of Marketing,* January 1965, p. 11.)

In the study of innovations, it is helpful to visualize the adoption process as consisting of a series of distinct but related stages. Behavioral scientists in their study of the diffusion of new products typically conceptualize the adoption process as consisting of the following five stages: *awareness, interest, evaluation, trial,* and *adoption* or *rejection.*

At the *awareness* stage, the individual first becomes exposed to the innovation either through impersonal or personal communications, but lacks complete information. He then may become *interested* in the innovation and seek further information about it. In the succeeding *evaluation* stage, the potential adopter appraises the innovation in the light of his present and anticipated future and then decides whether to try it on a small scale. After satisfactory *trial,* the tastemaker may finally decide to continue the full use of the innovation. However, the innovation may be rejected or discontinued at any state in the adoption process.

ASSOCIATION

Association is a simple but essential element, long discussed in many areas of literature. Essentially, two or more events or items are *associated* when from the prior experience of the respondent, one of them stands or relates to the other. Such a bond can result from similar or opposite association. This mental connection is thought of in a time or space contiguity.

Some behavioral scientists claim that thinking is really a process of association, one idea triggering another. Bonds between ideas are a product of experiences, sensory or reflective. As such, each individual's environment and experience bank are closely related to "what comes next." There is some minor reluctance to accept this hypothesis, since a person could conceivably become a bundle of dead ends. Yet ideas which are organized or related with some sort of meaningful bond are more easily remembered than those with no logical relationships.

Through common experiences or conditioning, many people exhibit similar association patterns. Because of this, some ad specialties have more universal acceptance in relating to the prime product or service the company offers.

ATTENTION

Attention is an essential factor for the advertising and personal selling functions in marketing. It is not easy to get initially and may be even more difficult to hold for any length of time. As such, it would appear that selling has a decided advantage in marketing communications, since many person-to-person techniques can be used to rekindle attention patterns.

In Brink and Kelly, *Management of Promotion* (Englewood Cliffs, New Jersey: Prentice-Hall, Inc., 1963, p. 104), attention is described thusly:

Attention is only a preparatory adjustment for further response, a setting of the strings of consciousness, a programming of the mind. An individual who has been adjusted to an advertising situation is in a position to make any further responses that may be desired; what will or will not occur depends upon the individual's characteristics and sometimes upon the act of accommodation in the sense organ employed—eye, ear, fingertips—which brings still clearer perception. This attentive state is also characterized by the dominance of one idea, image, impression, or a set of these and the subordination of all others. Consciousness always has a focal point, which, as pointed out earlier, is always occupied by that which is being "attended" at the time.

Specialty advertising items can be used to develop attention for a presentation or for the product or service itself. Furthermore, within the presentation process, attention at times must be concentrated on a particular product feature or process. With some ingenuity, a specialty item can help to meet this need for emphasis.

EMOTION

Advertising messages are generally oriented to appeal to human emotions. Some people employed in creative positions in this industry have, in the opinions of the authors, shown surprising talent in this area without evidence of having studied the subject in depth. But for a broader understanding, the inhibiting aspects of emotions must likewise be recognized and evaluated in promotional strategy. No party in marketing is immune from some degree of subjectivity, so a professional promotional counselor would also have to take into account the emotional force, positive or negative, of the specialty user. This could be quiet important in changing advertising effectiveness.

The role of emotion is appropriately discussed by Brink and Kelley (p. 91) as follows:

Emotions are difficult to analyze because they are subjective experiences. Although emotions are accompanied by certain psychological changes in the body (fear-sweating, rapid pulse, increased or decreased blood pressure, injection of adrenalin into the blood), the feeling that accompanies the emotion is experienced solely by the person having it. Psychologists cannot agree on how many different emotions are discernible. Many overlap—love and affection are degrees of the same emotion; rage and hostility are closely linked. . . . Regardless of the number, appeals to the emotions are used a great deal in selling and advertising. If the advertiser can arouse a strong emotional response and anchor his product or brand name to it, his message will receive attention and interest and make a deep impression.

LEARNING/MEMORY/RETENTION

Learning is an acknowledged complicated process, with scientists admitting they have not developed a full understanding of its forces or dimensions. In fact, eminent psychologists have proposed theories which are almost diametrically opposed. Some say individuals learn by combining parts to comprise the total of their knowledge, thus continually adding to a foundation that already exists. Others say that we relate in configurational wholes, that a total pattern is modified as a new factor is added to our knowledge. Here new information changes all relationships within the structure.

Learning, further, has been evaluated as intentional (efforts at education) and incidental (happenstance). This covers a broad range of individual differences which will not be covered in this book. But it is apparent that promotional efforts are directly concerned with the latter factor of incidental learning. Practitioners have long realized that theories of learning are related to their efforts when trying to successfully sell goods and services. Among these interests are questions of increasing retention through repetition, frequency and primacy of messages, timing and continuity of stimuli, and the element of participation on the part of communications audiences. Advertising texts persistently argue for the need for empathetic copy appeal, sharply defined product images, and a group appeal of togetherness (everybody's doing it). Contests and coupons, for example, are dependent for their success on the appeal of active rather than passive reception. The famous Jimmy Durante comment, "Everybody wants to get into the act," is more than a theatrical cliché.

Additionally, the retention or memory factor is of paramount importance. Attitude changes or behavioral inclinations are often temporary, and unless they are reinforced, a person is likely to revert to his original mental set. We describe memory, broadly speaking, as the way that a message is *received, stored,* and *recalled.* It is a description of one of our human activities, a part of our mental process. It is neither an abstract nor a concrete process at that, and all save those with organic malfunctions have some capacity to remember. Those who are concerned with understanding people should study this capacity—what stimulates memory, what is the human potential, and what are related roadblocks.

Classical studies have been carried out in this area for many years. Back in 1885, Ebbinghaus conducted research on the topic, and his work has been used as an example ever since. Repeated studies of regressive memory patterns substantiate his findings, strongly indicating that the *reinforcing* role of specialty advertising could be its biggest value in the promotional mix.

MOTIVATION

With motivation, we are again faced with the powerful interaction of several factors. Writers and scientists concerned with a description of motives or motivation must necessarily refer to needs and wants. When a need is realized by a person through sensing that a drive is not being satisfied, then a want or satisfaction-desire is created. Many levels of wants exist, but they all relate to basic motives which lie behind them. Motivation is therefore the energy source for people's actions. It becomes the why behind individual behavior and as such is a vital part of the foundation undergirding techniques and programs of persuasion. No advertising or selling professional can ignore what lies behind people's actions.

This energizing human factor is intimately concerned with almost all other variables in human behavior. It is basically a summary sheet for why people follow their particular action pattern. This relationship was well analyzed in *Promotional Strategy* (pp. 31–32):

(1) The study of motivation requires analysis of the relationship between *(a)* forces which energize behavior and cause man to act; *(b)* other factors which then intervene to shape the manner in which he perceives or "sizes up" alternatives available to satisfy these energizing forces; and *(c)* the results. It is the influences on perception which are of greatest relevance in promotion.

(2) Man is motivated by many forces, all of which work on him in different ways. The sum total of these influences at any point in time is

designated as the "psychological field." As the diagram . . . indicates, *needs* (many prefer to use the term "motive") initiate behavior. Then a number of additional forces interact to shape his perception of alternatives for need satisfaction and the resulting behavior. Certain of these factors are internal to the individual *(emotions, response traits, values, and attitudes)*. The social environment, however, also enters through *internalized social values* and through *social comparison*. Finally, a host of other influences might be noted such as weather. The goal or incentive chosen (i.e., the product or service), then, will be the one which offers a high probability of need satisfaction given the determinants of choice, and the resulting behavior will usually be *purposeful* for the individual.

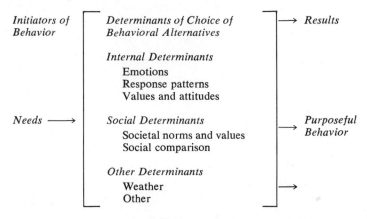

An individual's psychological field at any given point in time.

(3) Man generally does not behave in a random and capricious manner. Study of behavior over time presents the unmistakable impression that the "normal" person behaves systematically and consistently to achieve more or less clearly defined goals.

(4) The realization that man is subject to compound and often conflicting motivational influences permits a sharper understanding of the complexity of forces underlying behavior. Each individual must adapt to his unique psychological field and he will establish patterns of behavior which permit a workable and meaningful pattern of adaptation.

(5) The various motivational influences "set" the individual in a particular way so that he perceives those stimuli which are important to him. He is fully capable of "screening out" persuasive messages which are conflicting and this capability is frequently exercised to the dismay of advertisers.

An initial generalization emerges which is defended at length later:

Basic motivational influences render promotional efforts a contributing force which, at best, can only reinforce and redirect existing behavioral determinants. If major behavior change is produced, either these determinants are *inoperative* or they are *consistent with* and *in the direction of* the appeals in the promotional message.

NEEDS

Anthropologists have generally been associated with the science of identifying the primitive or primacy needs and how behavior patterns evolved to meet such needs. As society has developed, more attention has been devoted to psychogenic needs, that is, those needs that are not physiological in nature. Keeping in mind that, from a promotional standpoint, the needs of the purchaser, user, and influencing parties vary considerably for the same product, one can still group them for better understanding. First we have affection or acceptance needs, those involving love and belonging. Then we have ego enhancement, the factors of recognition, status, prestige, and achievement. Finally, we have defensive needs, concerned with anxiety problems, loss of face, or negative response avoidance. Some writers, on the other hand, break these categories into many levels for more specific examination.

It appears that specialty advertising can be used chiefly in the ego enchancement classification, with more limited use in the other two. But one particular trait, important to long-range sales success, offers unusual opportunity in marketing efforts. This is the "post-purchase" or "post-decision" anxiety experienced by almost everyone. In our present social-economic structure, there seems to be a growing need for reinforcement that a decision was correct. Perhaps this is due to the many more alternatives of choice now available, but people do look for a post-purchase rationalization that their action was the best and wisest they might have taken. If sales personnel or companies in follow-up efforts use a specialty item to communicate this concept and to add a friendly thank you, they will be filling a growing need.

PERCEPTION

People do not react to situations, but to their perceptions of these situations. As subjective factors are interposed on facts—experiences are brought in—the "set" of the moment comes into play. Thus, human behavior is not necessarily a reaction to external stimuli but more to the perception of these stimuli. To influence human behavior to any degree we must ask: "What can be done to add a different ingredient into an individual's internal processing system? If a person sees the world through the lens of his self image, to what degree can this inner self be changed or influenced? What are the major factors that determine this factor of perception?"

Because this topic is so important to marketing success, special attention should be given it by both practitioner and student. Of interest, therefore, is a quotation from an article by Donald F. Cox ("Clues for Advertising Strategists II," *Harvard Business Review,* November-December 1961, pp. 160–82).

We might consider these four conditions—exposure, perception, retention and decision—as the gateways to effective communication and persuasion.

Communications research has established beyond much doubt that the processes of exposure, perception, retention, and decision do not often occur at a random fashion among the population. To varying degrees, people are predisposed to expose themselves to certain kinds of communications and media and not to others. Different people tend to get different meanings from the same communication and to remember or forget different aspects of a communication. Finally, different people make different decisions as to whether or not they will be influenced.

Since each of these processes involves a selection or choice by individual members of the audience, we may refer to them as selective exposure, selective perception, selective retention and selective decision.

These factors have been studied and reported for many years. The common denominator between them rests on the observation that receivers exercise some control over what messages are received and retained. This is done through a choice of being exposed to communications in which people are interested or which are compatible to their desired physical environment. The converse is also true. People can avoid communications (except in captive audience situations) which are uninteresting, contrary, or irritating to their own convictions and opinions.

There is, furthermore, a selection process in the acceptance of a communication after the receiver has been exposed to it in an unavoidable circumstance. In fact, the original meaning of such a message may be drastically altered to conform to the listeners' or viewers' feelings. Retention of any message is similar. People filter messages, forgetting those which suggest incompatibility with currently held opinions, attitudes, or experiences. Since this is quite normal, any type of advertising cannot be expected to change an individual's behavior to a great degree unless the attitude is of little significance to the situation or not very strongly entrenched. Naturally, factors as changes in age, income, health, family situation, employment, or similar major influences are likely to alter people's predispositions rather dramatically. In such cases, attitudes are modified. Then, however, selective exposure, perception, and retention patterns are reestablished.

In *Promotional Strategy* (p. 39) these factors are referred to as important variables in a marketer's approach to demand analysis.

Selective perception has been found to take the form of: (1) distortion and misinterpretation of appeals to make them consistent with attitudes; (2) rejection of the source and messages as being biased; and (3) the communication of factual information but short-circuiting of the persuasive appeals. . . . The evidence on selective retention is by no means as plentiful as it has been on other selective processes, but enough is available to make it clear that the advertiser cannot overlook this possible reaction to persuasion.

REWARD

Rewards take many forms—tangible, psychic, physical, spiritual, and others. The motive to act a certain way for some return is still strong, however, and an individual does not necessarily have to sublimate this basic trait. Even if a person holds some motives in his subconscious, these do not have to be termed irrational or unreasonable. In fact, people purposely are prone to keep motives in the subconscious just because it's more comfortable that way, and less anxiety is created.

Specialty advertising is not as involved with direct reward as other elements of the promotional mix, but it is related and therefore of significance in studying consumer behavior. Sarnoff Mednik, in *Learning* (Englewood Cliffs, New Jersey: Prentice-Hall, Inc., 1964, p. 26) states:

Apparently all that is necessary for an association to develop between a stimulus and response is that they occur together frequently. Reward does not seem to be necessary. When reward is used, however, conditioning proceeds far more rapidly and with greater vigor.

If specialty items are used in the stimulus-response relationship, they may well over time become part of the reward associated with the pattern. (This point is covered later in the chapter more specifically.)

SET

Psychologists explain mental *set* as the readiness for an individual to react in a certain way to a given stimulus. The person actually expects a specific stimulus or stimuli and thus has his response ready. This phenomenon is common in relationships between people or between individuals and their environment. It also relates to perception, since a person has a tendency to perceive what he is set to perceive. Thus, even though a stimulus may change, the prepared response is forthcoming anyway. Almost everyone has had a personal experience in verbal dialogue when his or her comments, after thinking back, are virtually meaningless or not appropriate. "Thank you" is such a normal response that these words are spoken without thought. The mental set is such that this is just a natural reaction. The same situation develops when people greet one another. Words like "fine," "great," "yes" are sometimes used at will without relating to what is being said. Here one person is set with a verbal response to a verbal stimulus that never comes.

This has some unexplored ramifications for the industry, since inflated value could be placed on an item by the advertiser if the sole basis of evaluation depended on a word of "thanks" from the receiver. This response could be a result of set or conditioning on his part.

Ten commonly asked questions

1. What validity is there in the statement that the *giver* of a specialty item or gift also receives some psychic return in the distribution of such merchandise?

In the book, *Games People Play* by Dr. Eric Berne (New York:

Grove Press, 1964), lengthy explanation is devoted to the desire people have to give and receive some recognition benefits from each other. Dr. Berne referred to these as *strokes,* the stages of discourse development that two parties go through, changing, of course, as the situation and expectations are modified. The *giving* of any item not only provides the opportunity for such strokes (recognition units), but the merchandise itself may well represent some nonverbal stroke value. The giver needs feedback from the receiver. The type and degree of this response can be both positive or negative, but the giver generally receives something from the act itself.

2. Comments have been made that the act of giving or actual transfer of an item reveals something about the giver. What does this mean?

Chapter 4 explains the structure and methods of the industry's distribution system. Costs and time are naturally essential to consider in any strategy, but the more personal the art of giving can become, the more value the recipient feels the giving party attaches to the item or to him.

3. From the standpoint of behavioral sciences, is there an ideal advertising specialty?

It's doubtful if a completely ideal gift could be selected for any individual. Therefore, to fit the definition made previously for the content of this book where a message must be imprinted, a *group* would have to be considered as the recipient. Furthermore, any item would also be considered in regard to cost, method of distribution, competitive practices, and availability. Still, there are qualities which can make one item relatively more rewarding than others— practicality, novelty, frequent use, durability, pride or status identity, and a positive or happy consequence type of item as opposed to something which would suggest use in a negative situation (tear gas cartridge, accident identification tag, funeral director fans, etc.).

4. The word "novelty" has been used as a synonym for ad specialty. But as a descriptive adjective, what bearing does it have on the merchandise involved?

There is a basic trait of curiosity in all people. To say something is "novel" means it seems new or different. If such a quality can be added to other merchandise characteristics mentioned in the previous question, then all is well and good, but if this is the only appeal of the item in question, then there will be little lasting benefit to the advertiser.

Uniqueness or an unusual difference is a characteristic that has more durability. Almost all people become conditioned or used to something over time, so while an item remains different, it has the appeal of making the owner feel somewhat above those who don't possess a similar piece of merchandise.

5. What's the explanation of people wanting a second or third calendar or a tenth ballpoint pen?

Anthropologists have shown that in most cultures, people have a deeply ingrained drive to collect things. This trait goes back through the ages, relating no doubt to times when a scarcity of goods prevailed or people didn't know when the opportunity to replace an item would be at hand. Some clues are currently showing up that as an affluent society evolves, pride or need of ownership and possession may diminish.

Also, experience has shown that some items (like certain ballpoint pens) may have a quite limited life, and it's convenient to have another one handy. Most families likewise have many places within a home where they can use a calendar or where some writing instrument is needed.

6. Is there any evidence that an ad specialty should emphasize the company or product?

No conclusive answer can be given on this. Some experiments have, however, been conducted on very similar products in which brands have been switched around, and the respondents were unable to identify their previously strong preference for one particular product. This suggests in a very limited manner that the nature of the bond between the company and consumer is stronger than the nature of the bond between the physical product and consumer. It should be pointed out that these studies were done on food, tobacco, and health products, and that the differences between simulated laboratory experiments and the real world are usually very significant.

7. Can an ad specialty ever create a negative effect?

Yes. This is based on the premise that the greatest use of advertising cannot make a bad product acceptable or a bad image good, at least for long. If a person is reminded of a negative experience with a product or company, the item would therefore have a negative effect.

Advertising doesn't necessarily have to be believed in total to be influential, but if the imprinted message is quite inconsistent with brand claims or product performance, it can be negative. If the item is an insult to a person's self-intelligence concept or expectations of what his patronage is worth, then it may miss the target. If a man spends several thousands of dollars for a new automobile and his value as a customer is concentrated primarily on an imprinted key chain, the effect can be negative.

In addition, brand or company loyalty is rather difficult to define. Companies use "share of market" or "percent of repeat buyers in any given time" as clues to the answer to this question, so any conclusions as to how gifts or ad specialties contribute to repeat purchases could be challenged, based on what is presently known.

8. How does an ad specialty relate to habit patterns in purchasing?

Essentially, one must realize that most specialty items are not directly linked to a purchase. Their role is much more subtle than that of premiums or coupons. All people are of necessity creatures or habit, so humans tend to behave consistently in specific ways. As Walter A. Woods, in the *Journal of Marketing* (January 1960, pp. 15–19), pointed out, "Although it is unlikely that a given consumer always reacts in one way rather than another, people do react predominantly in one way rather than in other ways."

He goes on to identify six types of buying groups—habit determined, cognitive, price-cognitive, impulse, emotional, and new consumers. It's likely that ad specialty items would have more effect on the last three groups mentioned above, since in promotional goals it's not expected that imprinted merchandise should be the major factor in a purchase decision.

Habits are also involved with judgment criteria. Although the ad specialty industry is not too directly concerned with modifying habit patterns, it must be sensitive to the ways it can be of greater impact when used to complement other stimuli. Emphasis of product features that pertain to such judgment criteria is one approach. In *Promotional Strategy* (p. 41) observations are made that do have relevance to promotional counselors.

Most buyers acquire certain criteria which they use to predict product quality or desirability. For example, the color of maple syrup influences a judgment of whether or not syrup is thick or thin—the darker it is the thicker it appears to be. Similarly, Dove soap is said to have gathered a large market share because of its shape and feel. There appears to be an area of sensitivity at the point where the thumb presses the palm, with the result that one product is often preferred over another because of its feel in the palm. Finally, a large manufacturer of air conditioners found that one style of air conditioner case was overwhelmingly preferred by buyers in a preference test until it was disclosed that the case was made of a new form of plastic which strongly resembled metal in both appearance and feel.

All of these examples indicate that largely unconscious criteria were used to judge products. Everyone used judgment criteria that have proved successful in the past. For example, items made of aluminum are often rejected because they do not seem to be heavy enough; automobiles are rejected because the door slam appears to be "tinny." In a very real sense these criteria are a type of response pattern, because they are a determinant of the evaluation of alternatives for need satisfaction.

9. Are the reasons why ad specialties can be used for many different groups (customers, employees, dealer salesmen, stockholders, opinion leaders as examples) basically the same?

Yes. There may be relatively better imprinted messages in reaching one group as compared to another, but essentially, human behavior is *people patterns* and all of the above groups have some common denominators. Reference should be made to question number seven, since there are a larger number of ways to make mistakes when dealing with these groups. Strikes and labor problems would more than likely affect the strategy of the use of any merchandise. The same could hold true with stockholders if, say, profits were reported down.

10. If human behavior is so complex and dynamic, how can *any* information be current and meaningful?

In most instances in marketing and promotional planning, there is less need for knowing why a person acts or consumes than there is in finding out why things happen in *one particular way* instead of another. In this latter area, it is more a relative approach than an understanding of the total process. Also, the commercial orientation of business, especially marketing, must target on consumer and buying patterns.

This does not set aside the goal of understanding people in every possible way. As explained, all of the behavioral disciplines are intimately related. The study of factory production employees; of political, racial, or religious influences; or of educational trends are all vital and interesting. For the purpose of this book, the investigation is necessarily more limited. Yet there is a constant need for developing new, clearer, and more valid principles. This was succinctly stated by James V. McConnell (Ann Arbor, Michigan: mimeograph, University of Michigan Press, *Persuasion and Change,* 1959):

... to the social scientist, A's influencing of B is not a matter of art, but of the witting or unwitting application of known or unknown scientific principles, and must be looked upon as such. *The scientific analysis of human behavior is perhaps the single most potent weapon in A's arsenal.* If he fails to make use of this powerful tool, *he does so at his own risk.*

In closing this section, one other reference can be made to provide added insight for the promotional counselor and marketing student. It is to an artcile by Irving S. White entitled "Perception of Value in Products" (from *On Knowing the Customer,* ed. by J. W. Newman; New York: John Wiley & Sons, 1966), p. 103.

We can sum up the problem of the marketing of values in our economy in one sentence. Effective selling represents a constant realignment process between communicators of value and perceivers of value until an empathic dialogue occurs in consumption.

With all the dynamic factors in marketing, particularly the promotional mix, it's unlikely that any value relationship will remain valid and empathic for very long.

Finally, this list from *Human Behavior* is included for added consideration:

GENERALIZATIONS RELATING TO THE COMMUNICATION AND PERSUASIVE PROCESS

1. People tend to see and hear communications that are favorable or congenial to their predispositions. ...

2. Interest remains the single most significant determinant of exposure, and the major countering factor to self-selection of communications is sheer accessibility. ...

3. People interested in a topic tend to follow it in the medium that gives it the fullest and most faithful treatment.

4. The use, and perhaps the effectiveness, of different media varies with the educational level of the audience—the higher the education, the greater the reliance on print; the lower the education, the greater the reliance on aural and picture media.

5. People tend to misperceive and misinterpret persuasive communications in accordance with their own predispositions, by evading the message or by distorting it in a favorable direction.

6. The more trustworthy, credible, or prestigious the communicator is perceived to be, the less manipulative his intent is considered to be and the greater the immediate tendency to accept his conclusions.

7. In cases where the audience approves of the communicator but disapproves of his conclusions, it tends to dissociate the source from the content.

8. The nature of the source is especially effective in the case of ambiguous or unstructured topics.

9. People use their own changes of opinion, however recent or immediate, as blocks against further modification of opinion under the pressure of communications.

10. The effect of communication programs that try to convert opinions on controversial issues is usually slight.

11. The communication of facts is typically ineffective in changing opinions or desired directions against the force of audience predispositions . . .

12. The higher a person's level of intelligence, the more likely it is that he will acquire information from communications.

13. The more communications are directed to the group's opinion leaders rather than to rank-and-file members, the more effective they are likely to be.

14. Word-of-mouth or personal communication from an immediate and trusted source is typically more influential than media communication from a remote and trusted source, despite the prestige of the latter.

15. The explicit drawing of conclusions by the communicator is more effective in bringing about audience acceptance than relying upon the audience to draw its own conclusions from the material presented.

Source: Excerpted from *Human Behavior: An Inventory of Scientific Findings* by Bernard Berelson and Gary A. Steiner, © 1964 by Harcourt Brace Jovanovich, Inc., and reprinted with their permission.

6

Approaches to
special problems

To illustrate the diversity of uses of specialty advertising, this chapter will give specific case histories. Each of the cases will be approached on a problem-solving basis. Where possible, we will describe the original situation facing the ad specialties user, the establishment of objectives, the choice and use of a particular ad specialty to achieve the results, and the outcome of the application. Each of the illustrations took place sometime during the past five years. Pictures of the products, including the imprinting, are provided to give a clearer understanding. It should be borne in mind, however, that the product is secondary to the identification of the promotional problem, the creativeness, and the applicability exemplified in each case. Also, it must be pointed out that in most marketing strategy, all subsystems should be working well in concert. Success comes from a blend of all factors, and no one item should be given undue credit. Still, specialty advertising appears to have been a key ingredient in the following cases.

117

Traffic building

Kaiser Aluminum and Chemical Corporation of Oakland, California, was very interested in encouraging engineers in the automotive industry to utilize more aluminum trim on the automobiles they were designing and building. Even with only minor additions of aluminum trim per car, such applications, multiplied by the millions of cars produced, would represent a substantial increase in aluminum sales to the auto industry.

At a Society of Automotive Engineers Show held in Detroit, the company planned a way to draw the key buyers or influencers to its exhibit. In the exhibit, an Oldsmobile F–85 was being shown to demonstrate advanced uses of aluminum trim. To encourage attendance and interest, the company gave away the demonstration car in a drawing among top prospects who registered at the booth. In order to reach these men prior to the meeting, each of them was sent a Mylar pocket secretary made of material resembling aluminum foil. The Kaiser trademark was embossed on the front cover. Distributed by mail, the pocket secretary gave bulk and importance to the mailing itself, emphasized the dates of the show, served as an invitation to the hospitality party where the car drawing was to be made, provided a stub to be used for the drawing, and also registered the person as having attended the exhibit.

From the 912 pocket secretary invitations mailed, 308 invitees came into the exhibit, representing a return of better than 33 percent. Through a validation system, only recipients could register; thus all returns were from the people that Kaiser wanted to see. One Kaiser executive termed this SAE Show "the best we've ever had."

North San Mateo County
Board of Realtors

No. 3001

127 PARK PLACE
MILLBRAE, CALIFORNIA

Bank of America
SAN BRUNO BRANCH
465 San Mateo Avenue
San Bruno, California

90-904
1211

Date _____ Nov. 18, 1964

$1,000,000.00

PAY
TO THE
ORDER OF

JAMES PETTY, JR.

NOT NEGOTIABLE

James E Shaughnessy

Presented by U. S. Title and Guaranty Company

A sales conversation piece

Salesmen and buyers alike have seen so many different tie clasps and tie tacks that are promoting companies and their products that they have become almost indifferent to them. In order to attract attention, the design of such devices must definitely be something out of the ordinary.

To introduce a new product—instant gravy mixes—the Durkee Division of the Glidden Company, Cleveland, Ohio, chose a tie tack designed to resemble a gravy spot, with the brand name embossed on it. The slogan that went with the tack was, "If you must have a gravy spot on your tie, it better be Durkee's." Initially, the general manager of the Durkee Division had plans to present these tacks only at a board meeting of the parent corporation, but the reception there was so good that it was decided to use the specialty in the field. One thousands tacks were distributed to the salesmen. As they made their first calls on customers to introduce the new instant mixes, the salesmen wore the tacks, creating considerable conversation and serving as an excellent method of working the product into a sales presentation. All of the salesmen found good buyer response, and initial sales of the mixes were better than expected. In addition, three more orders were placed to fill requests for the tie tacks. Durkee considers this one of its most effective advertising campaigns in recent years, and many people, both in and outside the company, are still wearing Durkee gravy spots on their ties!

Starting a new business

When one begins a new business enterprise, it is necessary to attract as many new customers as possible so that volume is built up quickly. When a new enterprise was started in Concord, California, in addition to the usual types of grand opening gifts—ballpoint pens, yardsticks, etc.—the Concord National Bank wanted a promotion which would attract women depositors during specified hours on opening day. The solution created to solve this problem was a "fish bowl of money" and a transparent plastic tote bag imprinted with the words, "I grabbed this money from . . ." and the bank's name, trademark, address, and telephone number. Each woman opening an account of a specified size between 10:00 A.M. and noon or 2:00 P.M. and 4:00 P.M. was permitted to take a handful of money (mostly small coins) from the fish bowl, and she was provided with the plastic tote bag in which to carry her "loot." The reception of this idea far exceeded expectations. The number of new depositors was so great that the bank decided to run the promotion straight through from 10:00 A.M. until 6:00 P.M. without a break.

Promotion pays, both ways

Many companies find that their most effective advertising, that which is done on a cooperative basis with the retailer, is often not used frequently enough. The retailer, who generally has thousands of items to promote, may simply forget to incorporate certain companies into his advertising efforts.

Officers of the Dubuque Packing Company of South San Francisco, California, realized that they had to do something different to remind meat buyers in supermarkets of the Dubuque name, and so a series of mailings was prepared which would not require a lot of time to read and yet would be considered unusual and attention-getting. As its focal point, each mailing featured an ad specialty item accompanied by a rhymed message on company stationery. The jingle tied in with the advertising specialty, and copy on the specialty tied back to the jingle. As an example, for the mailing of a snap rule yeardstick, the following jingle was used:

> We know you'll be mighty glad
> If you run Dubuque Meats in your next ad.
> High public acceptance assures a demand,
> Which will make it outsell any other brand.
> Gain more profits each and every day,
> Feature a big Dubuque ham display.
> The enclosed snap rule sez with visuality:
> Dubuque brand is the Yardsick of quality.

The last line of the jingle was also used on the snap rule yardstick as the imprinted message. Other items used in the series included a clipboard, first aid kit, distance calculator, pocket knife, golf putting cup, circular chart, cost and profit calculator, and glass ashtray. These items were selected because they either tied directly into the job of the recipient or were related to his recreational interests.

Results were so good that the company planned to continue the promotion indefinitely. To the very pleasant surprise of Dubuque, many of the items have been requested in additional quantities by the recipients.

A tasteful reminder to busy people

Publicizing an industry to a group of newspaper editors is often difficult. Many other businesses are attempting to receive publicity coverage, so best results are achieved when the message is quite unusual.

Some 200 food editors, representing metropolitan newspapers of the United States and Canada with combined daily circulation of 60 million, were attending a Newspaper Food Editor's Conference sponsored by the American Association of News Representatives in New York City. To call the attention of these editors to its "Pineapple Impressions" press section, the Pineapple Growers Association used an advertising specialty that served as a continuing reminder for future pineapple promotions. Six "pineapple yellow" pencils, imprinted with a recipient's name, were bundled together, with one sterling silver pineapple charm attached to each bundle. The pencils, together with a teak pencil holder, were wrapped in tissue in "hot tropical" colors, boxed, and gift-wrapped in multicolored foil in the same colors as the tissue. Each package carried a die-cut label in the shape of a pineapple imprinted with "Very Special Person."

The editors, all women, were enthusiastically appreciative. Many sent highly complimentary thank you letters. In addition, many requested a second pineapple charm so they could have them made into earrings.

Fishing for business

Local media, including newspapers, television, and radio, often find it difficult to make their presence known to advertising executives located in distant business centers in the country. Yet they want to be known, so that when the occasion arises, they will be the first considered for reaching their respective markets.

Located in Orlando, Florida, Station WFTV outlined a four-step program. First, to announce that it is "Number One" in prime time in its market; second, to show that mid-Florida is the "Number Three" market in the state; third, to give a brief picture of the market; and fourth, to swell "WFTV-Powerful 9" identity with Orlando and the mid-Florida market. To accomplish these objectives, four mailings integrating a specialty advertising wall plaque were sent at three-week intervals to 415 top advertising executives throughout the United States. Each mailing was keyed to the theme, "Fishing in Florida?" and was fully integrated from shipping label to two-color die-cut promotional folder to wall plaque. The four plaques, in mahogany, carried brass figures of fish—dolphin, shark, tarpon, sailfish—and a brass plate reading WFTV—Orlando, Florida.

WFTV's national sales manager reported that "our fish plaque promotion appears to be the most effective and best received promotion we have ever done."

A cruel cut for competition

No one needs to be reminded that the competition for credit card business has been at fever pitch for the past few years. Many banks and other agencies have mailed unsolicited cards to entire metropolitan populations of people. What, therefore, can a company do to make its card stand out?

The American Fletcher National Bank of Indianapolis, Indiana, was the first bank in central Indiana to offer charge cards. As a result, their initial coverage was excellent. However, within a few months, their competitors began to flood the market with competing charge cards. In order to put across the idea that unsolicited cards could (and should) be destroyed, the bank distributed cardboard reproductions of its charge card with an imprinted key-shaped knife attached. The imprinted copy on the card read, "We don't want to fight . . . and you don't have to switch. Simply use this handy 'non-switch' blade to destroy credit cards that you don't need." Partly as a result of this effort, the bank managed to maintain its credit card customers, thus achieving its purpose.

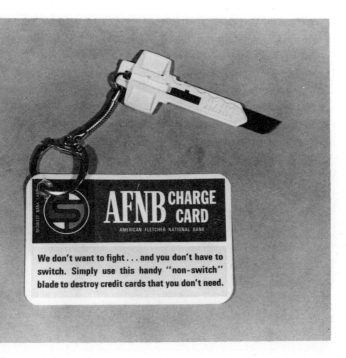

AFNB CHARGE CARD

AMERICAN FLETCHER NATIONAL BANK

We don't want to fight . . . and you don't have to switch. Simply use this handy "non-switch" blade to destroy credit cards that you don't need.

Specialties lead to ballooning profits

Although most plant managements believe strongly in the idea of getting production workers involved in quality improvement programs, few have found effective methods of doing it. Not enough of an air of excitement and urgency can be created in the average situation to make such programs successful.

Recognizing this, the Pitman-Moore Division of the Dow Chemical Company embarked on a program of total involvement of their 1,200 employees. The major purpose of the program was to revitalize the company's I/Q (Improve Quality) program and maintain a high level of participation. To inaugurate its promotion, a party was planned for all employees. Balloons, five feet in diameter, were used to call attention to the party assembly tents; banners were placed across driveways bearing the I/Q slogan, "Ideas in Action." On the day of the celebration, pressure-sensitive signs were placed in all areas of each plant, pointing out that "your ideas are important." During the following week, all employees were urged to submit a suggestion and receive an I/Q flower pen (400 proposals were received). Cafeteria managers began to use I/Q toothpicks and napkins; special coffee cups were put into service. I/Q ashtrays were placed in conference rooms and cafeterias. A flag was designed to be flown at the plant having the highest participation; a recognition program of plaques was instituted. I/Q umbrellas were used by secretaries; fluorescent flags were placed on fences; pocket protectors were given male employees and rain bonnets to female employees. An I/Q telephone dial ring called department managers' attention to the I/Q program. I/Q matches, bearing the slogan, "Be a Leader—Always Use I/Q," were placed in conference rooms and cafeterias; ashtray-coasters were provided employees for desk use; "tips and tolls" bags were provided for employees' cars. Lastly, I/Q balloons were used to create a party atmosphere in cafeterias.

In evaluating this program, Pitman-Moore attributes more than $300,000 in additional profit to that particular year's I/Q program, with additional benefits accruing in the following years.

Leaving a lasting impression with competition

It's important to the average company to be both respected and remembered by employees of its competitors. Yet whatever a company does in the direction of fostering such an attitude must be done well and in good taste to avoid hypercriticism.

Lincoln National Life Insurance Company of Fort Wayne, Indiana, has a large reinsurance department, and, during the course of any year, some 200 high-ranking executives of other insurance companies visit Lincoln Life to arrange for reinsurance. The firm wanted a high quality gift which would be kept and used by these top-echelon men, even though it was received from another insurance company.

The solution actually was found in the museum of the company —one of the finest Lincoln museums in the country. Capitalizing on President Lincoln's identification with the Civil War, a minié ball —a piece of ammunition actually fired during the war—was embedded in a lucite paperweight. Each executive was personally presented with a paperweight during his visit to Lincoln National. The gifts were enthusiastically and happily received and were found to be in use years after the presentation.

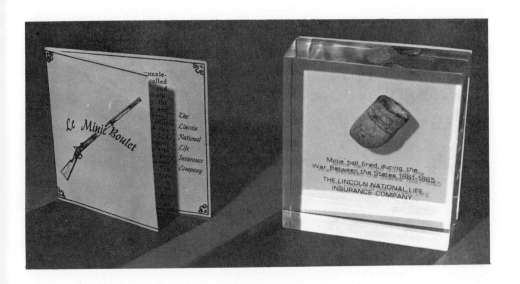

The magic sales approach

Choosing a device that seems unrelated to a product often helps dramatize the almost magic results of the product.

Chemical Engineering, a McGraw-Hill publication, wanted to provide company salesmen with an attention-getting device to help them sum up the sales points made in a recently completed direct mail campaign. To do this, *Chemical Engineering* salesmen handed their customers a "magic box" that contained the key to unlocking the industry's market. Usually the salesman would have to show the prospect how to open the box. Inside was a large key and chain that actually served as a key holder. Thus, with an air of mystery, the salesman dramatically demonstrated his sales message.

Results were highly gratifying. *Chemical Engineering* sold 519 more pages of advertising than it had the previous year, despite the fact that the magazine industry, as a whole, suffered sharp drops in advertising revenue during the same period.

Blessed results from specialties

Although it is highly unusual for a church to distribute advertising specialties, it has been done and with apparent success.

Trinity Baptist Church of Findlay, Ohio, felt that it needed to do something different to help boost membership. To do so, an ad specialties program was introduced to increase attendance, to generate enthusiasm for the church and make people want to come to church, and to motivate people to strive to live by the moral code set forth by all religions and especially those of the faith of Trinity Baptist. The church used ad specialties to commemorate holidays as well as to achieve particular aims during the year. For instance, on Mother's Day, all mothers were given book markers, key chains, sewing kits, and flowers. Imprinted pencils were given to visitors to fill out visitor cards, and appropriate specialties were given Sunday School children throughout the year. One Sunday, children were given helium-filled balloons to release after the service; the person who found the balloon which had traveled farthest received an airplane ride.

Results are partly demonstrated by a comparison of growth before and after the program. At the end of its first 13 years of existence, the church had a membership of 50 families. After three years of using advertising specialties, membership has grown to more than 300 families. On the 12 Sundays during which specialty advertising promotions were conducted during 1968, attendance increased between 25 percent and 50 percent over the previous year's figures.

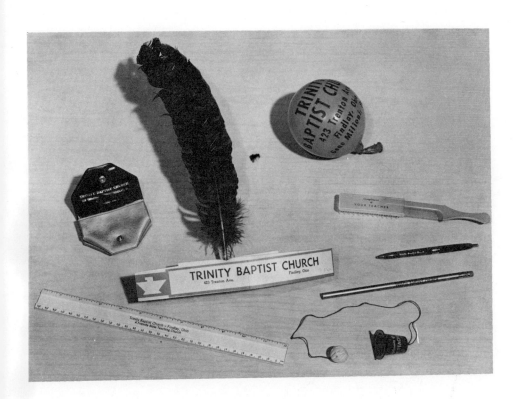

Summary

Throughout all of these examples, attempts have been made to illustrate the wide diversity of application and use of specialty advertising. Note that the *idea* is the critical dimension. Often the same or similar ad specialties are used over and over; but each time, they are presented under a new set of circumstances, with a new set of objectives, and therefore they result in a new set of outcomes. Creativity is thus the paramount factor, just as it is in the application of any promotional technique. Selection of the item is comparable to the choice of the illustration to be placed in the print ad. But exposure to the ad specialty will be magnified hundreds of times over the print ad, and this exposure will be much more selective, specifically reaching the desired audience.

As in the print ad, one may have a number of general objectives in mind when applying specialty advertising—everything from simply creating awareness about a company and its products to actually inducing action to buy. These general objectives, along with the program's specific objectives, must be carefully thought out before one can ever hope to choose an appropriate item from among the thousands of ad specialty items that are available. Planning, therefore, is as important to specialty advertising application as it is to any other phase of marketing. Also, it should be reiterated that all parts of the marketing and promotional efforts must be related, coordinated, and then carried out with maximum effectiveness.

7

Environment in the marketing mix

THERE are strong indications that the amount of change in this industry in the next decade may well surprise many of its leaders. It could be significantly greater than the total changes in the industry over the past quarter-century. For a greater sensitivity to the forces of change, a brief examination of the environmental forces is considered appropriate at this point. This will serve as background for the concluding chapter in which some of the things most likely to take place for the industry in the next decade will be identified. A brief summary is also found at the end of this chapter pointing out how specialty advertising relates to these major points.

No one time segment is independent of what has preceded it, and it is vital that people learn from any mistakes or inopportune decisions of the past. Further, what is taking place at the moment will very shortly be identified on many trend lines as just a point in time. So looking back helps to determine in which direction our economy and society is headed.

Ten years ago as our country began the decade of the "soaring 60s," a major theme in business and marketing literature centered around the tremendous significance of the population explosion. Perhaps some of the writers and prognosticators were carried away by their own enthusiasm regarding the quantitative charts they created. People by the numbers were here, and people meant customers, and customers meant success. Optimism was rampant, and it was felt that any company or industry with average talent was virtually bound to succeed.

Some defunct companies in industries closely related to numbers of people can attest to the fallacy of this single premise. Furthermore, society has abundant testimony that even though the quantitative aspect of our population went up, so did the qualitative problems. Some of these problem areas are related to the decreasing significance of the individual as numbers increase. "Where do *I* fit into the system?" has become a common question.

With all signs indicating even greater levels of population by 1980 (although perhaps at a decreasing rate), the individual's need for singular identification and recognition is likely to grow correspondingly.

Estimated and projected populations: 1960 to 2020*

YEAR	Series B	Series C	Series D	Series E
1960	180, 684	180, 684	180, 684	180, 684
1965	194, 592	194, 592	194, 592	194, 592
1969	203, 213	203, 213	203, 213	203, 213
PROJECTIONS				
1975	219, 101	217, 557	215, 588	214, 735
1980	236, 797	232, 412	227, 510	225, 510
1985	256, 980	249, 248	240, 925	236, 918
1990	277, 286	266, 319	254, 720	247, 726
1995	297, 884	283, 180	267, 951	257, 345
2000	320, 780	300, 789	280, 740	266, 281
2005	347, 073	320, 055	293, 751	275, 066
2010	376, 249	341, 033	307, 436	283, 711
2015	407, 379	363, 191	321, 683	291, 893
2020	440, 253	385, 959	335, 869	299, 177

* In thousands. Estimatee as of July 1, 1970. Includes Armed Forces abroad.
Source: *Statistical Abstract of the United States, 1970*, Table 3, p. 6.

Government

Another factor closely conected to this will be the continuation of the present trend for groups in society to turn to the government for solutions to their needs and problems.

As an example of "local protection laws," New York City has recently passed a consumer protection act. Among the statute's provisions are powers enabling the city to prosecute any individual or company that victimizes the public by means of deception in business dealings. Class actions can now be instituted on behalf of consumers. Fines are significant against any person or business found guilty, and the subsequent publicity is bound to have a widespread effect on the future of any party involved.

It is not our purpose to do more than observe that greater involvement of government—at *all* levels—in business is bound to have direct effects on business practices, marketing and communications, and therefore, on specialty advertising. The following observations in an article entitled "New Battleground—Consumer Interest" by Tom M. Hopkinson, in the September–October 1964 issue of the *Harvard Business Review* (p. 100), may sum up the situation for the next decade as far as government involvement is considered:

1. As evidenced by consumer agitation at the local-state-federal levels, business has failed to meet the total needs and desires of today's consumers.
2. Into this business-created vacuum, government forces have quickly moved to answer this consumer need.
3. The areas of consumer interest are so diverse that they offer government agencies and legislators almost limitless reasons for additional regulation of business and commerce.
4. If business managers want to avoid such new government regulation (with the attendant possibilities of excessive and punitive legislation), they will have to take positive action to demonstrate that the business interest is in more general accord with consumers' needs and wants.

It is point number three which holds the greatest significance as it relates to Parkinson's Law, which posits a make-work philosophy. Considering that at local, state, and especially federal levels of government there are thousands of employees whose jobs depend on existing or new controls or restrictions on business, it is not surprising that this trend is expected to continue. The pros and cons of such activities are, of course, important, but it is only relevant in this context that we acknowledge what lies ahead. Laws often follow marketing or consumer/user areas of interest. This may be due to neglect or lack of consideration of the total interests and activities of all parties involved with the manufacture and distribution of products or performance of services, but it also relates to especially strong political motives, since the popularity index of consumer protectionism rates high in voter appeal.

Governmental linkage to personal income is historical. Furthermore, as minimum wage laws are passed or expanded, they are quite likely to affect a large number of sales personnel of distributors in the industry. Those sales people who work part-time have been helpful in building the aggregate industry volume, since it is they who in large part have called on the small volume users. Changes in this area could radically affect the structure and methods of the industry.

CONSUMERISM

For even more background, it is important to note that some proclamations often precede social understanding or acceptance by 10 to 20 years. Such a suggested "manifesto" was published back in 1962 by Colston E. Warne. This is undoubtedly a subjective viewpoint and involves one side of a broad and delicate subject, but the thoughts expressed by Warne are far more commonly accepted now than when originally published. Since they are in the area of advertising and particularly relate to major mass media, it is important to consider them.

A CONSUMER MANIFESTO

Herein lies the need for a consumer manifesto which would include as a minimum the acceptance of the following basic elements:

1. The new communication media—radio and television—were not created for advertising. The airwaves are owned by the consuming public; and the costs of radio and television, whether indirectly assessed through advertising or directly through the cost of electricity and television acquisition and maintenance, are consumer costs. Advertisers are there incidentally as nonpaying guests in the home and are not to be obnoxious, long-winded, stupid or inane. Program content is rightfully not the creature of the advertiser, dedicated by his dictates to cater to the lowest common denominator of mass taste.
2. The countryside belongs to the consumer, not to the advertiser.

There is no inherent right to create incessant affronts to the human eye every hundred yards along a highway—a procession of billboard slums.

3. Newspapers and periodicals have their central responsibility to their readers, not to their advertisers. This responsibility is compromised whenever dubious standards of advertising acceptance prevail or where choice is warped by planted stories designed to sell, not to inform.

4. Legislative and self-regulatory efforts to impose truth in advertising and to ban false and misleading advertising, although possessed of great merit, have thus far proven notoriously ineffective. They need to be improved. No prohibitions on false advertising, however drastic, can suffice to compel advertising to play its essential role in our culture. Truth in advertising is not a residue left after the elimination of falsehood. Advertising has ever been prone to discover new techniques of subtle deception whenever prohibitions have been imposed. What is needed today is the application of a supplementary approach.

5. Specifically, a policy is proposed of *caveat venditor*—let the seller beware—a policy to be enforced by our social and legal institutions. An advertisement should be a warranty to the purchaser of the price and quality of an article. Thus, the burden of proof as to an advertising claim will lie squarely upon the seller or a branded good. A claim should be accurate and complete as to all essential details, and should constitute a full disclosure of both the merits and demerits of the good in its intended use. Advertising should not be poised on the slippery edge of irrelevance, misrepresentation, or deception. The obsolescent and socially destructive idea of *caveat emptor* should be appropriately buried as a relic of the days of simple markets and well-understood commodities.

A very current viewpoint on this was supplied in an article appearing in the March 1970 issue of *Premium Merchandising* published by Merchandising Publications, Inc. New York City, in which Maurice Stans is quoted:

These are some of the basic rights of the consumer which I believe we must all acknowledge: First, the consumer certainly must have protection from fraud, deceit and misrepresentation. Second, he must have access to adequate information to make an intelligent choice among products and services. Third, he must be able to rely on products working as represented. Fourth, he must have the right to expect that his health and safety will not be endangered by his purchases. Fifth, our marketing system must provide him with a wide range of choice to meet individual tastes and preferences.

Even more significant are observations which are being made by knowledgeable and influential advertising practitioners. Introspective industry analyses are taking place, objectives are being questioned, and methodologies are being challenged. The following represents some present analyses and comments of marketing executives:

QUOTES FROM PRACTICAL ADVERTISING MEN
David Stewart, Kenyon & Eckhardt Advertising Agency:

. . . there are four facts about modern advertising, which, taken together, are highly disturbing . . .

1. Advertising has become far more necessary to U.S. business than ever before . . .
2. Advertising has become far more costly . . .
3. Each dollar of expenditure returns less in sales results than it did a few years ago.
4. Advertising . . . has become bogged down in red tape, in systems, procedures, viewpoints and operating methods which prevent it from doing a meaningful job.

He indicated that businessmen have a responsibility to the entire economy to eliminate advertising waste and inefficiency.

Clarence Eldridge, retired Vice President of Marketing, General Foods:

It may seem paradoxical to imply that the influence of advertising is declining at a time when expenditures for advertising have reached an all time high.

1. With respect to a great many categories of products, there is no substantial difference between competitive products.
2. The believability of advertising is being seriously jeopardized by the attempt to create "psychological differences," psychological superiorities, in products where no such differences or superiorities exist.
3. The sheer volume of advertising . . . there is too much of it.

Source: Comments from speeches given before the National Retail Merchants Association as reported in "Progressive Grocer," *Progress,* July 1964, New York, pp. 1–2.

ECONOMIC FACTORS

One important aspect in the economic picture is the rate of increase of disposable personal income, particularly the segment available for discretionary purchasing. It is in this area that the competitive efforts of marketing activities will be intensified. It is interesting to note that disposable personal income between 1950 and 1960 went from $206.9 billion to $350 billion, a 68 percent increase. From 1960 to 1969 (preliminary figure) there was an additional increase to $629.7 billion, or another 80 percent.

Relation of gross national product, national income, and personal income and saving: 1950 to 1969*

ITEM	1950	1955	1960	1965	1966	1967	1968	1969 (prel.)
Gross national product	284.8	398.0	503.7	684.9	749.9	793.5	865.7	932.3
Less: Capital consumption allowances	18.3	31.5	43.4	59.8	63.9	68.6	73.3	77.9
Equals: Net national product	266.4	366.5	460.3	625.1	685.9	725.0	792.4	854.4
Less:								
Indirect business tax and nontax liability	23.3	32.1	45.2	62.5	65.7	70.1	77.9	86.6
Business transfer payments	.8	1.2	1.9	2.7	3.0	3.2	3.4	3.6
Statistical discrepancy	1.5	2.1	−1.0	−3.1	−1.0	−1.0	−2.5	−6.2
Plus: Net subsidies of govt. enterprises	.2	−.1	.2	1.3	2.3	1.4	.8	1.1
Equals: National income	241.1	331.0	414.5	564.3	620.6	654.0	714.4	771.2
Less: Corporate profits and inventory valuation adjustment	37.7	46.9	49.9	76.1	82.4	79.2	87.9	88.7
Contributions for social insurance	6.9	11.1	20.7	29.6	38.0	42.4	47.0	54.4
Plus: Govt. transfer payments to persons	14.3	16.1	26.6	37.2	41.1	48.8	55.8	61.9
Interest paid by government (net) and by consumers	7.2	10.1	15.1	20.5	22.2	23.6	26.1	28.7
Dividends	8.8	10.5	13.4	19.8	20.8	21.5	23.1	24.6
Business transfer payments	.8	1.2	1.9	2.7	3.0	3.2	3.4	3.6
Equals: Personal income	227.6	310.9	401.0	538.9	587.2	629.4	687.9	747.2
Less: Personal tax and nontax payments	20.7	35.5	50.9	65.7	75.4	82.9	97.9	117.5
Equals: Disposable personal income	206.9	275.3	350.0	473.2	511.9	546.5	590.0	629.7
Less: Personal outlays	193.9	259.5	333.0	444.8	479.3	506.2	551.6	592.0
Equals: Personal saving	13.1	15.8	17.0	28.4	32.5	40.4	38.4	37.6

* In billions of dollars. Prior to 1960 excludes Alaska and Hawaii.
Source: *Statistical Abstract of the United States, 1970,* Table 478, p. 315.

In the area of discretionary spending, the alternative use of consumer dollars will be disbursed over a rather broad spectrum. Competition will subsequently increase as more industries are involved. Not only will companies have to communicate and market within their own industry, but they must also be sensitive to all possible ways for the consumer to spend these available extra funds. Costs of competing in a broader area will be greater, so more return will be needed per dollar invested in advertising and promotion. This necessitates a closer examination of where the funds go and which combination of media mix brings the greatest return. Properly understood and merchandised, specialty advertising can turn this trend to its advantage.

Closely associated with this factor is the predicted increase of leisure time available to our population. Some forecasters have been quite positive in their statements, and a few have even suggested a work week as low as 25 hours by the end of the 1970s. Other writers seem less inclined to reduce working hours to this level. But there does seem to be a consensus that the trend in this direction will continue.

This movement will not, of course, be universal in our economy. Management responsibilities may even have a tendency to increase as a direct result of reduced hours by production-service segments of industry personnel. If this trend is continued, it could become an accepted pattern by a greater number of people, as forces push toward some general conformity of personal efforts as they relate to goals and rewards. This, too, would affect the methods and tools used to reach groups with advertising messages.

If greater leisure time likewise has a relative effect on travel, hobbies, outdoor recreation, and the like, specialty advertising can take another step in reaching its potential volume, for it is one medium which can be used as a direct link with home products and services as people travel and use convenience items carrying advertising messages.

Turning more specifically to the marketing area of our national economy, a major trend is the growing service segment of our economy. Yet in spite of the acknowledged increased importance of this area, there is still a lack of information and valid research being done. Part of this may be due to inherent problems of service marketing. To mention a few factors: lack of service standardization (i.e., as compared with products); lack of an identified pricing system in many areas; the high personal aspect of many services; the localized aspect of service availability; the "manager-owner" characteristics; extra difficulties involved in doing research (common problem identification, universe determination, sample selection, data gathering, etc.); the inadequacy of pertinent records; the newness of many services; and, the dearth of management knowledge and experience and particularly literature beamed to the service industries.

SERVICE INDUSTRIES

Regarding the last point, many marketing texts and journals, when mentioning the service industries, make the statement that in marketing the same principles that apply to consumer products likewise apply to services. Similar comments are made regarding the relationship between industrial products and services. This approach is taken primarily because at the moment there is so little knowledge to the contrary.

During the next decade, this is quite likely to change. The research challenges are becoming tempting and inviting to marketing researchers and practitioners alike. The growth of some service industries, a higher degree of coordination through association efforts, the need for better information by new service chains, and the need to effect economies and increase efficiency in service industries— all will cause greater emphasis to be placed on analysis of the service marketing system.

How does this relate to specialty advertising? According to the members of the Specialty Advertising Association International (SAAI), the industry is essentially oriented toward the service industries. In 1966, SAAI conducted a survey among its members asking whether to continue to *gather and publish certain data* which were broken down according to various industries and subgroups. This survey was a valid study and resulted in over a 20 percent response. Of the top 10 groups recommended to be retained in the published literature, 7 were strictly of service type industries and 3 were a service-product combination classification.

One section of the same survey further related to groups the members considered their best customers. The report stated:

Perhaps the most interesting and informative findings of the survey are found in the tabulations of the question concerning the categories in which the distributor personally experienced the "best sales."

Distributors were asked to rank their own best sales category as number 1, the second best as number 2, the third best as number 3, etc. These rankings were converted to ratings. The category ranked number 1 by a distributor was given 10 rating points, the category ranked number 2 by the distributor was given 9 rating points, the category ranked number 3 by a distributor was given 8 rating points, etc. The total points were added in each category and then divided by the number of distributors mentioning that particular category resulting in a "rating" on the category.

The rating assigned each category is an expression of interest of a selected number of distributors. It would have been entirely possible for a single distributor to be the only one to rank a particular category as number 1 thereby giving that category the ultimate rating of 10.0. In this survey CAMERA STORES and JEWELRY STORES were tied for the fewest number of distributor mentions at 12 each.

BANKS and SAVINGS AND LOAN ASSOCIATIONS received the highest number of distributor mentions.

Multiplying the category rating by the percentage of total distributors mentioning, produced an end figure (eliminating the decimal) which is indicative of the "strength" of one category as compared to another. BANKS with the highest distributor rating multiplied by the percent of distributors mentioning results in the highest category "strength" rating of 512.

The top 10 in this analysis reported 6 as strictly service and 4 as service-product classifications. Furthermore, the one new group added for future publications was the insurance industry, another service-oriented group. Perhaps the specialty advertising industry can be accused of being fixed on the past and neglecting the gathering of information on product groups that offer an increased sales potential in the future. This is understandable, however, since consumer products have been more traditionally oriented toward premiums, which is presently another separate segment of the promotion mix. This segment has its own trade association, but there is growing evidence that this separation won't be as distinct in 1980 as it is today.

BRANDS

Another important aspect of marketing is the area of branding. During the coming decade it is highly likely that the role of branded merchandise will change somewhat. Present trends already show that private labels controlled by major retail organizations have made inroads into share of market on a regionalized basis. Large manufacturers with their own branded merchandise are involved in this since in most instances they manufacture or produce the same private labels. These manufacturers have likewise established second and third brands within the same line, depending largely on differences in grades or standards, prices, outlets, or even consumer group differences (i.e., age brackets).

Some authorities feel the brand picture will get more complex, not only due to efforts by manufacturer or middlemen, but also because of changing purchasing patterns. Patronage support of a retail outlet, either through direct purchase or by the increasing use of catalogs or direct mail folders, can change the relative role of national brands. This, along with the potential upgrading in vending purchasing patterns, tends to make the selling process less personal. It is important to watch whether this will shift a greater part of the selling function to advertising and promotion. Customer and user mobility is still another factor which tends to affect the previous historical methods of moving merchandise. As one marketing man aptly observed, "The old merchandising walls are rapidly crumbling."

Obviously if the burden placed on the advertising and the communications mix is increased, this should increase the opportunity to involve special and different approaches. But since this primarily involves products, specialty advertising practitioners will have to reexamine how they can enhance the value of their marketing contribution.

This leads into another vital and more subtle aspect of the purchasing process. Here specialty advertising's role is more apparent. Some studies have been made in this area, namely the proliferation and changing influences of the purchasing decision. This concerns both products and services, although consumer and industrial product studies have been much more extensive. It is important to note that in the case of retail stores for example, the original decision to add a line or product is the one that is the most difficult to influence or analyze.

When more people are involved in any purchase decision, the salesman must alter his presentation and sales appeals to a greater degree. In many cases, those involved in making the decision do not personally face any salesmen. Product or service information must be relayed in printed material or by other members of the purchasing group. Thus, any idea (translated into a merchandise reminder) to reinforce a product benefit, sales appeal, or point of interest becomes increasingly important in the sales communications process. Here is a decided opportunity for specialty advertising, even if in limited volume.

In certain instances, part of the purchase decision is being put on computers to evaluate the capacity for a product or company to meet minimal standards. In fact, in reordering various staple consumer products, the entire process has been programmed for computer analysis and decision. This is inevitably going to be a more common pattern in the future, which will necessitate even greater supplier efforts to get initial product acceptance. As mentioned before, specialty advertising will have the opportunity to become much more of a part of a total sales effort than has been the case up until now.

BUDGETS AND COSTS

One important trend of the 1960s, increasing to an even greater degree as we begin the 1970s, is the improved analysis and determination of advertising budgets. As previously mentioned, for years business has used a mixture of guesswork, percentage of sales, a fixed figure per unit sold, and subjective judgment. Now some companies and industries have introduced budget systems based on the marketing task to be accomplished or a return-on-investment figure. New approaches are bound to come and will be related to a synergistic mix and the results of media model testing. All of this will, of course, be tempered by any new legal restrictions or allowances in regard to product and service claims, media used, or possibly a fixed budget figure based on the amount of gross sales volume.

Changes will not come quickly. There is controversy currently in professional advertising and promotion circles regarding the method of charging for services. Commission and fee arrangements are not uncommon within the same agency in fact, based somewhat on profitability of an account or the acceptance of a fee agreement by the advertiser. It's natural for a professional agency to relate more positively to a medium which is a source of income, vis-à-vis the mass media. However, if a larger number of agencies use a fee for services base, it can be expected that they will be able to devote more attention to a wider spectrum of advertising and promotional methods or tools by which their clients' marketing goals can be reached. It stands to reason that as any consideration is given to broader ways to promote, specialty advertising will receive more attention.

In conjunction with agency change, even the basic role and structure of agencies are undergoing major modifications at this time. The increase in independent time-buying services, although posing some new problems of vested interests and compensation, may well be part of a trend of specialists in the mass advertising professions. Within a few years, the business community could have people engaged almost exclusively in budget counseling, scientifically thought out and tested. Development of creative service agencies has increased too, so the advertising field is itself in the midst of some significant realignment.

From a marketing standpoint, advertising practitioners in the professional ranks could well use a form of specialty advertising in their own promotional efforts. Among the worst promoters in the business world are companies and agencies that sell promotional advertising services. This may be because such a small part of agency income is budgeted for promotion. Nevertheless, more firms are likely to see the results of neglect of "using what they sell," as they are subjected to increasing examination, criticism, and restraint.

FRANCHISES

Franchises have grown rapidly, and have even perhaps reached oversaturation in some fields. When a franchise development is successful, the buying pattern that emerges is one with a centralized purchasing department. Franchised outlets buy from headquarters, and all promotional efforts are related and coordinated. Many members of the specialty advertising industry have had the experience of seeing a local independent customer join a franchising operation and, subsequently, buy all his specialty merchandise from the main office of the franchiser. This makes the competitive situation more difficult, not only for companies or shops in direct competition with the franchise outlet, but also for suppliers trying to get an order from the central purchasing department.

The industries in which franchising has enjoyed the greatest success have been those in which product or service identity has been possible. At times a well-known person has been the anchor for this step. But it is difficult to envision this as a major development for the benefit of the specialty advertising field.

A more logical development would be the evolution of a stronger pattern of selected or limited distribution by suppliers. This could also be a step taken by the stronger distributors, which, for them, would be a move away from the marketing definition of general merchandise wholesalers. Currently, some distributors in the industry are closely akin to sales agents, sales representatives, or brokers, but if the distributors are large enough, a buying committee could be used to select the type and width of the product line. This is not a supplier selection approach, but it is oriented to picking specialty items closely associated with the distributor customers' needs.

RESEARCH

Demographic data procural has been significantly refined. New types of information are being collected, analyzed, and used. Developing banks of psychographic data (although being questioned by some able research people) is a new step. The capacity to store and retrieve information has increased tremendously. Developments in use of zip-code research plus the voluminous data made available following the 1970 census will materially affect research efforts and results. Assimilation of this additional data and their effective use in planning marketing strategy should not be done precipitously, however. It may well be that some information will never be used. Nevertheless, the existence of improved information systems in a competitive environment will virtually force the acceptance and use of better methods, and this is bound to be translated into changes in evaluating advertising effectiveness and promotional alternatives. This could be specialty advertising's best opportunity to make for itself a more significant place in promotional strategy.

COMPETITION

Most industries in the course of the next few years will find themselves confronted by new competitors. Not only will this competition come from newly created companies, but also from presently established organizations which are expanding into new fields. As this occurs, the present advantage time enjoyed by any one company will be affected. This is, in fact, one of the most subtle yet powerful forces working in our economic structures today—the shrinking of advantage time. Almost all studies call for this to continue in the market place.

This premise holds especially for features used in product differentiation, in packaging innovations, in sales strategy, in price advantages, in distributive channel activities, and in advertising appeals and promotional strategy programs. Business is sensitive to the forces working to make the product life cycle shorter, from introduction, through growth, through the maturity phase, and ultimately the period of decline. It is more than ever necessary to devote greater effort and attention to the prolongation of product service life.

SUMMARY

What does this all mean to the specialty advertising industry? Some comments on this have already been made in this chapter, and the following chapter will deal more specifically with what can be expected in the next decade, but a few generalizations as to what the environmental factors could mean in a longer range perspective are worth repeating here.

Population growth. Trends are up, which brings a strong desire for individual identity. A feeling of resistance could develop against anything which is part of a mass. Something special, something a bit different and more individualized will have greater appreciation and value attached to it than formerly. The specialty advertising industry could find this to its advantage.

Governmental involvement. SAAI, like all other groups, will have to continue to be sensitive to any activity that could be interpreted as restraint of trade, price fixing, or even causing consumer or user duress. But the individual members of the industry will also have to be sensitive to their own customers' (the advertisers) use of merchandise items. Over-claims or false claims in advertising will be more effectively singled out.

Discretionary spending and leisure time. Competition for increased discretionary spending power and the accompanying growth of leisure time will increase significantly. Old companies and industries will expand to get a share of this growth, and new companies wil be started. This will result in a far greater choice of opportunities for the consumer in spending both money and time. Many special user groups will be started and identified. It will not be feasible or profitable to reach them with mass approaches in promotion, so special campaigns, special appeals, and special media will be used.

Services.   Much more research, organized strategy, and coordinated efforts will be exerted to improve marketing efforts of services in the future.

Promotional mix.   Special ways will evolve to promote private brands, not only those of retail chains but also some which are being merchandised from retailer to retailer. The hitherto casual use of specialty items at company sales meetings may be modified as sales managers use them to promote or reinforce themes of meetings, selling techniques, or product benefits. Trade shows will probably continue to use ad specialties to emphasize product features to purchasers.

Research.   The long-range implications of improved research hold great promise for all marketing activities. The expected identification, separation and subsequent analysis of consumer segments has great significance for any medium that can be used to reach these groups.

8

Some thoughts
about the future

Iₙ attempting to envision the developments of the next decade as the specialty advertising industry may be affected by them, it is appropriate to quote from an address given by Israel Margolies at the Specialty Advertising Association International, Sales Management Practices Conference held on March 17, 1966 in Chicago, Illinois.

Techniques, methods, ideas considered avant garde only yesterday are obsolete today. What is true of every industry, every field, is no less true of our own. . . . In the specialty advertising field, it may well be educate or dissipate, evaluate or disintegrate.

It depends upon whether advertising specialties are sold as gimmicks, giveaways, something everyone does, or if they are sold as part of a planned program designed to accomplish specific objectives.

In refining our thinking and defining our purpose, . . . we will have elevated our industry to its rightful place among the major media of our country. But more important, we will have strengthened and secured for ourselves the economic basis for our existence. . . . It is high time every salesman in our industry knows *why* he is selling, not just *what* he is selling; and every buyer knows *why* he is buying, not just *what* he is buying.

It is not likely that specialty advertising will, within the next decade or two, be considered as a major advertising medium, since by the very nature of being special, ad specialties are supposed to be different. But specialty advertising does have an important role to play and the potential for even greater industry sales exists.

Changes are taking place in and around the industry, not all of which are consistent or strictly positive in regard to specialty advertising. For an understanding of the direction of this industry, several major points must be considered.

Broadly speaking, management and control of change should be the order of the day. There are indeed more technical, more affluent, larger, and newer segments of our economy which involve greater innovation and change, but there are also a number of industries where the potential for change is not as great and where the leadership is more prone to remain closer to present operating methods. The specialty advertising industry is making serious efforts to become more involved in the total communications system. Energies are being directed toward becoming better known, and business in general has increased its attention to categories or areas of expenditures which were previously thought of as miscellaneous or unclassified.

Some of the industry's leaders, on the other hand, have been quite justifiably concerned with its growth relative to the entire economic picture. This feeling was expressed by George L. Curran, ex-chairman of the board of the SAAI, who spoke at the Annual Membership meeting of SAAI, on March 15, 1967 in Chicago.

My personal evaluation of our industry development is not one of growth, but one of loss. Sure, we have grown in total dollars since 1910. We have a lot more people in our industry. But what has our growth been when compared with the economic growth of the country or the dollar growth of other forms of advertising?

CHANGING ROLE

An important factor is the changing identity or role of specialty advertising. Some spokesmen claim that the industry is closely linked with advertising per se, creating acceptance of the product or service and thus drawing products through the channels by invigorating user demand. Others say that the industry is more closely associated with promotion, some draw but more push. Young leaders in the industry tend to feel that it makes no difference, that in the role of creative counseling it can be both. This at least is an acknowledgement that a broader involvement with change can be expected in the years ahead by younger industry members.

PREMIUMS

There is also evidence that the overlapping of premium and specialty advertising is increasing. It's not so much what people in either industry would like to see exist or what association efforts are made to set up a definite line between the two; the key is what the buyers or users want. Currently some items are being imprinted with a manufacturer's name or logo and sold as premiums in conjunction with attendant purchases. In fact, in limited instances an accompanying purchase is not even necessary. Here one finds a definite erosion of the traditional differences between specialty advertising and premiums.

For an advertising specialty company to pass up an opportunity for sales, an expanded involvement in the broad spectrum of promotion, or greater opportunity and capacity to serve customers can prove to be short-sighted strategy. Premiums and incentives are big business, with well over $4 billion in annual sales. And premium suppliers are increasingly imprinting their items and selling directly to ad specialty customers.

The percentage of total incentive business now sold by specialty advertising companies is negligible, except for business gifts. But since both incentive or push-type promotional plans and advertising specialty programs occasionally use the same or similar items, the differences then hinge on the conditions of receipt. The companies using the merchandise are rightfully interested in the ideas, the service, and the program and have little concern for any supplier's desire to be classed in a particular industry.

One more obvious difference between the markets for premiums and specialty advertising centers on conventional commissions paid to the sellers. Serving the premium market brings far less commission, generally between 5 and 10 percent. The far greater volume, however, makes the sales effort worthwhile. But, in addition, it is highly important in premium selling to have a close knowledge of the customers' merchandising and distribution problems in order to develop the necessary promotional program. Target groups should be specific, goodwill objectives should be spelled out, and the steps necessary to receive the premium should be easily understood. Yet since premium suppliers range from a small manufacturer getting rid of surplus inventory via a self-liquidating plan to a premium division of a major corporation, this professional approach is not always apparent. The common channel in advertising specialty selling from supplier to distributor to client-advertiser is much less rigid in selling premiums, although more flexible in the capacity to serve smaller customers and fill smaller orders.

SALES PROMOTION COUNSELING

Sales promotion has been defined by the Sales Promotion Executives Association (SPEA) as "any activity which increases or speeds up the flow of goods and services from the manufacturer to the final sale." In studying the promotion mix, the mass media (TV, radio, print) are not included. Under this concept it is quite easy to include specialty advertising as a part of the spectrum of sales promotion. The professionally classed sales promotion agency performs under this wider spectrum of services, involving the agency in publicity, display advertising, premiums, some research, contests, direct mail, merchandising or retailing activities, and general campaign administration. To be able to perform satisfactorily involves a wide variety of special knowledge—including the role that specialty items can play in reaching specific goals. No commitment to any particular part of the mix should be used. Rather the optimum use of any medium is employed to reach promotional objectives.

Many marketing activities could become part of the sales-counselor service mix. For example, early in 1969, Carl Rosenfeld, on retiring from the board of directors of SAAI, posed the following question:

... perhaps we should turn toward the complete sales promotion approach and include in our market strategy services which we now shun: market survey, direct mail, point of purchase and premiums. Many, if not most of our distributors and suppliers have entered one or the other of these fields in recent years.

Looking ahead, the strongest surviving companies 10 years hence will have embraced a policy of offering a broader spectrum of service. Past and present attempts to define the industry within narrow concepts will still be continued, but in practice, progressive companies will go beyond the parameters that the industry now uses to describe itself. One of the reasons will be the entry of new people without concern for present practice or tradition. A decade from now, we will quite likely find among the industry marketing leaders both men and women who have entered the industry from advertising agencies, other media, sales agencies, or retail and service concerns. Even now there are talented and creative concerns in the industry. But in a decade there should be more, with less clustering around similar approaches to merchandising and counseling. This may actually result in fewer organizations in 1980 than exist today.

SOCIAL CHANGE AND RESTRAINTS

In the total economic picture, it's difficult to see the industry challenging or greatly influencing social change. Yet, as a growing part of the promotional mix, it must become more involved than at present. The current trend was well expressed back in 1961 by R. Eells and C. Walton in *Conceptual Foundations of Business* (Homewood, Illinois: Richard D. Irwin, Inc., 1961, p. 37–38).

In the contemporary scene, business is no longer the institution playing a subordinate role in the mighty drama of events. It has achieved in the secular societies of the West some stature of partnership with other value-forming institutions. Perhaps business has the potential of becoming for our time a "force civilisatrice." For, as it provides the goods and services that makes possible the good life for a greater number of people, it crosses, in peace, those frontiers where religious differences (Moslemism versus Christianity) or political differences (communism versus democracy) have hitherto made any neutral amity impossible.

Another factor must, however, be considered. For the past 10 years we have witnessed an increase in the number and vocal activities of many self-appointed social and economic reformers. This characteristic has become popular politically and has gained recognition for activists who otherwise would be devoid of attention. Examining the trend, it is apparent that many of the reformers want the improvement beamed essentially at other parties. No group is exempt from a psychotic fringe segment, not even lawyers, educators, writers, ministers, or scientists, and especially not any part of the political body.

The activities of these people unfortunately tend to overshadow the activities of many conscientious people who objectively point out positive need for improvement and who in turn suggest ways to do just that. Here we find also an element of practical thought, recognizing that when one change comes about it is indeed likely to have a ripple effect for others. Among such people are found businessmen who recognize the place that gifts have played in all the history of man's relationships. But they also know that overemphasis on this can bring about negative net results. A decade ago an article entitled, "How Ethical are Businessmen?" appeared in the *Harvard Business Review* (July–August 1961, p. 100) in which business executives listed practices they would like to see eliminated. At the top of this list appeared the classification, "gifts, gratuities, bribes, 'call girls.' " There can be many interpretations of this report, and it may be that a relative factor enters, that is, "gifts above a certain amount." Our own government, for example, at the highest level bestows gifts on dignitaries around the world. But it must still be recognized that gift giving is a practice that will periodically be scrutinized, criticized, and questioned as to value. It can be expected that legislation regarding giveaways, contests, and direct-mail promotions will be persistently introduced at national, state, and even local levels. The industry cannot ignore this situation. It must consistently try to place gifts in the proper place and perspective in human relationships.

INDUSTRY SALES PERSONNEL

One of the most prevalent comments within the industry today is for the development of an aggressive, creative, and capable sales force, oriented toward a service approach to customers. This problem must be analyzed from the standpoint of the supplier and of the distributor. As explained in previous chapters, in spite of common goals, a dichotomy exists between supplier and distributor for which there is no simple answer. Distributors as merchant middlemen brokers carry out the complete sales function for many suppliers. Collectively, their success is vital to the latter group, but individually this is not so. They cannot legally act in concert against a supplier; nor could this be done feasibly even if it were legal. Little strength is concentrated anywhere in the industry, including suppliers and particularly distributors. Their primary attention is on competitive activities within the industry.

This may well be the main reason why the SAAI is persistently asked to take some action or make some recommendation which could quite easily be interpreted as restraint of trade. The authors saw instances of this in a number of situations. It was obvious that the men involved were not cognizant of the legal ramifications of their requests. But this inward look and negative approach is still a strong factor in industry practice.

Recognition that competition for sales personnel is primarily with other industries is essential for executives in specialty advertising. Unless action is taken on this within the next few years, the industry is likely to suffer even more than it has in the past. A few companies, with leadership that can conceptualize this need, could well set the pattern, but it is difficult now to identify where in the industry this will happen. To compete successfully, certain changes will have to be considered.

Compensation and recruitment.   The industry is largely oriented toward straight commission while the majority of American businesses pay on a type of salary-bonus plan.

Changing this would not only alter the security factor of entering and remaining in the selling function of the industry, but could even more importantly shift the emphasis away from merely selling merchandise to a more truly promotional counselor role. If the industry wants younger men and women who have been brought up in an environment that has placed more emphasis on security up to a certain minimal level rather than greater long-range opportunity, then this must be given deep consideration.

The amount of income made available to people being recruited into the industry is another important variable. There has always been a close relationship between the level of talent attracted and the income offered or realistically expected. Specialty advertising could not be labeled as a "glamour industry" when compared with the space industry, television, financial institutions, computers, and a host of others, so the industry's executives should become more sensitive to what income is being offered, particularly to younger men and women, by all of American business.

Regarding an organized system of identifying the best sources of recruiting sales personnel, at present no industry pattern exists. There is the normal amount of mobility *within* the industry, together with distributors bringing in younger personnel through affiliation with small family enterprises. The pattern for suppliers is somewhat different. Since many of them also produce merchandise for other segments of the retail or promotion industries, they are less likely to be bound by current specialty advertising industry tradition. Very inconsequential efforts are made toward finding personnel at educational institutions. A significant percentage of the new blood that exists just seems to drift into specialty advertising. Some of these men and women are quite successful, but such a pattern does make for a high rate of turnover. A transit type of sales personnel means that those on the move continue to move until they seem to find their place or can't move on. Quite naturally, many of the more talented sales personnel become distributors, thereby contributing to the weak image of the state of selling that remains.

Training and development.   Some salesmen in the larger firms do receive exposure to training programs. This is especially true of suppliers, but often distributors depend on marginal efforts by the suppliers, or they revert to the archaic method of providing catalog sheets and samples.

In the next few years, more progressive suppliers and distributors will avail themselves of sales training made available through their associations, adult educational courses, programmed training packages, programs sponsored by various marketing professional associations, and those made available by companies specializing in this service.

PRICING

Traditional patterns in which the producer sets the price and communicates this to the end-buyer through catalog sheets is not unique to this industry. The strategy has been to relate costs to what the market place will bear, with the distributor normally doubling his cost to establish the ultimate selling price. This discount arrangement can bring about overpriced merchandise in spite of quantity discounts. Here is the seed of distributor price-cutting, since this type of selling not only becomes possible but also inviting.

With price instability, it therefore becomes more normal in a wide spectrum of American business for the customer to go directly to the producer. In the specialty advertising industry the link of producer-user is especially strong since the supplier knows all users, as well as their buying volume, from having filled imprint orders. If it weren't for the fact that distributors provide the *new* markets and customers for suppliers, the direct channel of producer to user would likely become more popular.

One of the most significant steps that could be taken to change the image and role for this industry in the promotional mix is in the area of distributor pricing policy. If, indeed, the industry's members can become marketing specialists geared to produce ideas and promotional themes, then such creativity should have a *monetary value* beyond the merchandise used. It is likely that some companies with confidence in their capacities will actually apply this charge to a greater degree in the next ten years. Some distributors even today will not sell certain merchandise until they see how and where it is to be used. They pass up certain orders rather than see the specialties misused or off target. But such situations are rare.

True, most marketing ideas can't be protected by legal means, but buyers are becoming more sophisticated and are more likely today to value the concept of idea generation than a few years ago. If the service idea emphasis is an integral part of the sales presentation, the buyer has to be aware that the selling company puts a value on its time and proposals. Therefore, before the end of this decade we may see distributors' sales organizations put a monetary value on any segment of their time. If unusual counsel and service is rendered and the subsequent merchandise is ordered from another source which has contributed nothing and which received the order strictly on a price-cutting basis, then the first company can prove its contention that its time has value by rendering an invoice for the time spent. Some may say that in selling any product, every call has an element of risk that the selling time will be wasted if the order is not received. This is normal in all selling—products and services. But the growth of *professional* services and the obvious trend that labor charges in services are being accepted, strongly suggests that the specialty advertising industry should consider this step. What would be lost? Nothing, other than the possibility that the next call made on the customer would provoke some questions.

What on the other hand could be gained? A better understanding of the promotional counseling concept on the part of the buyer, since a specific value would be attached to ideas, plus a higher status for the creative distributor. Some strong feeling exists that ingenuity and service is the basis for optimism about the industry's future. This approach would help to establish this viewpoint. It must be remembered that ingenuity should not be confined to new products, new uses, or new methods of specialty distribution; new ways to improve the output of the total promotion mix should be of equal importance.

Selective distribution

The ease of entry into the distributive area of the industry has resulted in a disproportionate number of small marginal companies. Possibly for the short run this can assist a supplier in reducing excessive inventory, providing payment is received for the merchandise. But no industry can claim this as a long-range strength.

Some might say that a more stringent screening of distributors could result in concentrated power and control, or that it is against the American tradition, which lets anyone get started in business. The industry is so far from this situation, however, that the point is hardly worth further discussion. Furthermore, entering an industry which has marginal operations increases risks and makes success much more difficult, so sentimentalism in this case is redundant.

Suppliers don't have to establish exclusive distributorships. A selective policy can be used. Furthermore, classifications of distributors could be established according to the width of services performed, types of markets served, annual volume, merchandising functions performed, and similar criteria. By doing this and substantiating the value of certain distributors, one could justify price concessions through the channels. The end of this decade will probably see some suppliers using this approach, although it will take more marketing cost analysis, more research, sharper strategy, and increased courage. Distributors too are likely to develop a more selective approach to suppliers. This is, of course, done now by informal evaluation of supplier service and product quality. But it's possible to be much more analytical if quantitative values are attached to important factors such as (1) speed and reliability of communications concerning inquiries, (2) sample rebate policies, (3) flexibility of operations, (4) reliability in confirmation of orders, (5) speed of equipment to imprint orders, (6) high standards of imprinting, and (7) innovative nature of items offered.

Market segmentation

Probably the greatest opportunity for the specialty advertising industry to make impressive progress will center around segmentation. Mass media are becoming more segmented and thus more targeted. But even more significant will be the continued efforts on the part of specialty users to segment their markets. As this is accomplished, the promotional thrust will be more toward the rifle approach and away from the shotgun approach. If the industry can capitalize on this trend, it should have a very significant effect on the growth pattern.

This type of marketplace development could have another dimension. There are changes that develop from the customer through the channel to producer. As segmentation becomes more important, it might force deeper understanding per segment and a sensitivity to the best promotional combination to reach it. Thus a closer understanding of the relationship of ad specialties, packaging, point-of-purchase, direct-mail, and premiums will be necessary.

Miscellaneous observations

Some industries have either volunteered or been forced into a type of ingredient or product standard. For example, there are various grades of leather, vinyl, imprinting materials, and other things that are important to product acceptance. This is one development which will receive increased attention by the specialty advertising industry in the next decade.

Since no companies dominate the industry, SAAI's function is quite important to any progress that lies ahead. This organization will have to continue to provide services such as management development seminars, public and government relations services, research activities, selling opportunity identification, and so forth. In fact, these types of programs should be expanded as the industry develops momentum and growth.

Market segmentation will not automatically bring success to any company within the industry. Research and analysis are prerequisites. A better grasp and understanding of a market segment in order to stress the purpose of a specialty is essential. Concurrent with this is a full understanding of how to maximize benefits through the best method of distributing the item. This involves packaging, since a piece of merchandise can often be elevated from the give-away to the gift classification merely by being put into a box.

Some of the younger men in the industry have a better sensitivity to the need for such a research approach, knowing *what* and *how* to do research to get answers for improvement. A few suppliers are currently using computer services to assist in inventory control, selecting cost and pricing information, and customer buying patterns. This technique will become more sophisticated and will be expanded to include a variety of new data banks in the next few years. Once this is done, the competitive pace of the industry will pick up and affect other activities.

As such developments occur, it is quite possible that the specialty advertising industry will come into its own era of assimilation and mergers. As pointed out, there is a scarcity of large and influential companies for an industry with such a total sales volume. It's quite likely that a conglomerate company could buy into the field and subsequently grow quite rapidly by buying organizations to obtain national coverage of major markets. It's even possible that a national organization could be developed at the promotional counseling level through the use of franchise market expansion. The services that such a chain could offer would relate premiums, gifts, ad specialties, internal company incentive merchandise, items used by direct sales forces, and other uses for merchandise as it relates to people motivation.

If the industry were activated by such an event, its image would, of course, be altered. In fact, it may take something like this to change advertising practitioners in other media and in agencies who may not otherwise modify their feelings about specialty advertising. They are presently too preoccupied with some powerful challenges to their own function, status, or service. Even though they now work in an environment which includes calendars, gift desk sets, lighters, pens, ash trays, memo books, desk pads, and matches in waiting rooms, some agency men still question the worth of specialty advertising. It may take younger men advancing through the professional ranks to bring the greatest acceptance of synergistic marketing strategy, marketing cost analysis, market segment research, and other important decision tools necessary to understand the value of specialty advertising.

1980

It is highly likely that 10 years hence many of the same observations being made today will still be valid. Improvements will nevertheless come as progress is made within the industry. Many companies that fail to change to some degree will lose their relative strength. Those that identify the opportunities in the forces that have been discussed and then take action have an optimistic decade ahead. The authors realize that every industry has some members whose chance to change is limited, but many more where a reluctance to change prevails.

For some of the present senior members of the industry who are prone to look with concern, unhappiness, or uneasiness at critical statements by younger members of the industry, the authors suggest the following analogy. The example involves a dialogue with a country club manager located in a Midwestern state whose comments parallel similar ones overheard in this industry. The transposition to specialty advertising practitioners' concepts is not difficult.

The statements made by this club manager could be summed up as follows: "We're not planning any changes for a long time. . . . our income is adequate. We're not going to raise dues because we don't really need any more money. . . . our members are happy. They represent successful executives and their families, ranging in age from their late forties on up to their late sixties, and a few beyond that. . . . our employees have been with us for years, outside of the younger group of service personnel who generally don't work anyway and who are always jumping from job to job. . . . our location is excellent, right on the edge of town, generally accessible to members who live primarily in suburban homes. . . . our physical facilities are relatively superior. No major changes or additions are considered at this time. . . . our 'service-mix' fits our members, so why should we bother this."

The picture that emerges is satisfaction and complacency. Businessmen often think the same way, merely using other terms such as "gross sales volume," "profit," "prospects and customers," "sales and service personnel," "location of retail outlets," "width of product or service selection," "competition," and "innovation." The major point of emphasis is that regardless of whether or not any organization desires to preserve the status quo, the forces beyond the control of the group are so powerful that this becomes an impossible objective.

Here are some facts.

Adequate income.　In a sense adequate income means fixed income or annual income that meets present needs. Ignoring the forces of inflation could be fatal to any enterprise. Thousands of elderly citizens who retired and felt reasonably secure 10 years ago can attest to the fallacy of "not needing more."

Happy members or customers.　Happiness is a relative thing for all users and buyers. Such a temporary state certainly can be reached, but this can be quickly changed when compared with other products or services that bring greater benefits or value returns. Even conditioning can enter in, since when people assume they will enjoy or receive certain things over time, unless some changes or modifications are made, these benefits tend to lose their meaning.

The second part of this "member or customer mix" relates to age. Even if the total group could remain the same with no attrition, the aging process changes needs, benefits, or the capacity to use products or services.

The same "senescence" factor applied to employees. For the business owner who complains that he has to pay "a boy in a mail room $2 per hour when I started at $5 a week," the only reply is that he should do his own mailing.

Location.　Any facility that is presently located on the immediate outskirts of town, within one decade will be surrounded by people and physically related to an entirely new environment.

Competition.　For the businessman who feels a vested control over a group of customers, the observation can be made that in 10 years he'll not only have direct competition from another organization catering to his present group, but new enterprises will be working to get more of the customers' attention, time, and money.

Any specialty advertising concern that feels complacent, that will not face the uncontrollable forces of the environment, that accepts status quo as the best alternative, not only won't survive, but will have difficulty justifying its existence through the decade ahead.

The marketing student who is considering areas of opportunity for service, being involved with change, interesting challenges, and a better than normal chance to innovate quickly should consider the specialty advertising field as an area to invest his or her time, talent, and energy. There are a number of progressive firms in the industry that are willing to lead, to invest in younger men and women, and whose goals indicate a desire to grow and build.

Appendix A

A principal purpose of this book is to provide background information on which further investigation and research can be based. In any discipline, it is usually the accumulation and building of knowledge which is identified as progress rather than revolutionary advances which may come unexpectedly. Many possible practical and academic projects are suggested as one studies this industry. Some are more feasible as association efforts. Others are more oriented to experiments under controlled conditions and consequently could be part of academic graduate research.

Some answers are suggested in this book, but more specific quantitative approaches could add valuable knowledge. Furthermore, any subsequent study would reveal possible trends, which, of course, could be the basis of more valid conclusions. Questions which might be explored and thereby contribute to the body of knowledge in specialty advertising and promotion are:

1. What does the use of specialty advertising add to direct selling efforts? Can this assist in paving the way for a sales call or increase receptivity in a sales presentation?

2. Does the use of specialty advertising add specific traffic increments in trade or other commercial exhibits? Is this a valid marginal cost? Concurrently, does the use of such items increase traffic in permanent type show rooms, or add any qualitative benefit as sponsor identification, product information, or sales message retention?

3. To what degree does the use of specialty advertising items increase response in: (a) marketing research projects, (b) consumer contests, (c) use of dealer assistance programs, or (d) alleviation of post-decision anxiety?

4. Can specialty advertising be used and to what degree in: (*a*) changing attitudes regarding products, (*b*) proper use of products, (*c*) product awareness in new product publicity, and (*d*) any advertising task like copy or theme identification?

5. How can saturation or reduced effectiveness in use of any specialty item be identified and evaluated?

6. Can the role of specialty advertising be identified and studied in regard to community activities and/or plant tours?

7. Is there a use for specialty advertising in increasing productivity or participating in suggestion systems for employees?

Appendix B

FOR the benefit of those industry members who want more acquaintance with models and systems analysis of advertising decisions, we include the following model by Julian L. Simon from his article "A Simple Model for Determining Advertising Appropriations" in the *Journal of Marketing Research* (Vol. 2, No. 3, August 1965, pp. 286–87). Realize that this is a specific analysis, not extremely sophisticated and probably to be modified as other variables are justified and added. Many students are already acquainted with this or a similar model and shortly will be using such aids in their own analysis and decisions. It would be remiss to assume that we are on the verge of reducing all decisions to quantitative formulas, in spite of what some polarized educators may think. But it is equally myopic to ignore any scientific tool which can add to the effectiveness and efficiency of management decisions.

MODEL FOR GENERAL ADVERTISERS WITH SMALL MARKET SHARES AND A RELATIVELY UNDIFFERENTIATED PRODUCT

We shall assume that the firm for whom we are constructing the model is small enough so that its advertising expenditures will not elicit "defensive" expenditures by other firms; that is, the firm's appropriation may be set as if other firms' advertising will not be changed in response. Furthermore, the small firm's advertising for a product that is not physically differentiated competes for sales against other firms, rather than against the same firm's advertising in other periods. (Later this assumption will be loosened to deal with larger firms.) Our firm may sell either an expensive durable product, *e.g.,* a washing machine, or a repeat purchase item, *e.g.,* bread.

The dependent variable will be "net revenue," R, equal to total revenue minus cost of goods sold, delivery costs, and other non-selling variable costs. We shall assume that these deducted "production" costs are a linear function of output. This assumption is not likely to vitiate our conclusions over the ranges of operation we shall consider.

Let

T = advertising period $(T = 1, 2, \ldots m)$, .

t = revenue period $(t = 1, 2, \ldots n)$,

$T = t$

$R_{T,t}$ = net revenue caused by advertising in period T, realized in period t, undiscounted (gross revenue less all production costs).

$V_{T,t}$ = present value net revenue

A_T = Advertising expenditure in period T

P_T = profit from advertising in period T

b = retention rate, equal to 1 minus the decay rate of customer purchases from period to period (in absence of further advertising)

ρ = discount rate of the cost of money to the firm

$\sum_{T=1}^{t} R_{T,t}$ = sum of sales in period t, caused by all prior advertising in periods 1, 2, … t.

By definition, the total sales in period t, $\sum_{T=1}^{t} R_{T,t}$, are the sum of those sales attributable to advertising* in period T, plus the sales that would occur in period t even if no advertising occurs in t. The latter may also be thought of as sales in period t caused by advertising in all periods prior to T. Therefore:

(1)
$$\sum_{T=1}^{t} R_{T,t} = \sum_{T=1}^{t-1} R_{T,t} + R_{T=t,t}.$$

By definition of the retention rate,

(2)
$$\sum_{T=1}^{t-1} R_{T,t} = b \sum_{T=1}^{t-1} R_{T,t-1}, \text{ i.e.,}$$

---

* Assume that we are dealing with a firm in which the sales caused by advertising can be logically partitioned from sales caused by other factors. In some cases, such as cigarettes, advertising may actually be the prime mover of sales.

sales in the present period caused by prior advertising equal sales in the last period diminished by the decay rate. So

$$(3) \qquad \sum_{T=1}^{t} R_{T,t} = b \sum_{T=1}^{t-1} R_{T,t-1} + R_{T=t,t}.$$

the sales caused in period t by A_t are

$$(4) \qquad \sum_{T=1}^{t} R_{T,t} - b \sum_{T=1}^{t-1} R_{T,t-1}.$$

It is this core idea upon which the model is built.

It is known that the sales caused in period $t + 1$ by $A_{T=t}$ will equal $R_{T=t,t}$ diminished by the decay rate, $(1 - b)$. Similarly, sales in $t + 2$ will equal those in $t + 1$ diminished by $(1 - b)$, and so on, *ad infinitum*.

The basic result of this model is then:

$$(5) \qquad \sum_{t}^{\infty} R_{T=t,t} = \left(\sum_{T=1}^{T=t} R_{T,t} - b \sum_{T=1}^{t-1} R_{T,t-1} \right)$$
$$+ b \left(\sum_{T=1}^{T=t} R_{T,t} - b \sum_{T=1}^{t-1} R_{T,t-1} \right)$$
$$+ b^2 \left(\sum_{T=1}^{T=t} R_{T,t} - b \sum_{T=1}^{t-1} R_{T,t-1} \right)$$
$$\ldots + b^{\infty} \left(\sum_{T=1}^{T=t} R_{T,t} - b \sum_{T=1}^{t-1} R_{T,t-1} \right).$$

In other words, the total sales caused by advertising A_t in all periods equal the total of the sales caused by A_t in each future period; this is true by definition. The sales caused by A_t in each future period equal the total sales in that period, less sales that would have occurred anyway.

Since the terms within each bracket are identical, the entire expression can be simplified to:

$$(6) \qquad \sum_{t}^{\infty} R_{T=t,t} = \frac{1}{1-b} \left(\sum_{T=1}^{t} R_{T,t} - b \sum_{T=1}^{t-1} R_{T,t-1} \right).$$

So all that is needed to estimate the total sales caused by A_t are sales in $t - 1$, sales in t, and the retention rate.

To allow for the diminished value of a dollar in revenue in the future, as compared to current revenue, we modify with the discount rate. The *present value* of the advertising in the present period, $A_{T=t}$, is then obtained.

$$(7) \qquad \sum_{t}^{\infty} V_{T=t,t} = \frac{1}{1-b\rho}\left(\sum_{T=1}^{t} R_{T,t} - b \sum_{T=1}^{t-1} R_{T,t-1}\right).$$

The profit from advertising in the present period is:

$$(8) \qquad\qquad P_T = \sum_{t}^{\infty} V_{T=t,t} - A_{T=t}.$$

This enables us to compare the profitability of given advertising levels, assuming we know the sales in each period, the sales that would occur during this period with each given level of advertising, and the retention rate. The most profitable level of advertising can then be selected by inspection. This simple idea is the main finding; apparently, it is the first time it has been so stated.

The profit-maximizing rule can be expressed thus: advertise until

$$(9) \qquad\qquad \Delta A_{T=t} = \Delta \sum_{t}^{\infty} V_{T=t,t}.$$

To illustrate, assume a firm with:

Retention rate b from year to year $= .65$

Last year's sales

$$\sum_{T=1}^{t-1} R_{T,t-1} = \$1,387,000.00$$

This year's sales

$$\sum_{T=1}^{t} R_{T,t} \text{ for } A_T \text{ of } \$564,000 = \$1,289,000.00$$

Discount rate $\rho = .90$

The value in sales of this year's advertising equals

$$1,289,000 - (1,387,000 \times .65)$$
$$+ \qquad .65\,[1,289,000 - (1,387,000 \times .65)]\,.90$$
$$+ .65 \times .65\,[1,289,000 - (1,387,000 \times .65)]\,.90 \times .90$$

etc.

As a shortcut, calculate

(10)

$$\left[\frac{1}{1 - .90 \times .65}\right] (\$1,289,000 - .65 \times \$1,387,000) = \$929,000.$$

This example is based on 1960 data from Palda's study of Lydia Pinkham. Similar computations for years before 1960 are shown in [the] Table. The retention rate of .65 is an approximation based on Palda's estimates. The discount rate of .90 seems appropriate for a small business, such as Lydia Pinkham.

TABLE

APPLICATION OF ADVERTISING MODEL TO LYDIA PINKHAM DATA

(1) Year	(2) Sales in t caused by prior advertising, in thousands of dollars	(3) Advertising in t, in thousands of dollars	(4) Profit from advertising, in thousands of dollars
	$\left[\dfrac{\sum_{T=1}^{t} R_{T,t} -}{d \sum_{T=1}^{t-1} R_{T,t-1}}\right]\left(\dfrac{1}{1-bp}\right)$	$- \quad A_T \quad =$	$\sum_{t}^{\infty} V_{T=t,t}$
1960	387×2.4	564	365
1959	484×2.4	644	518
1958	312×2.4	639	110
1957	492×2.4	770	411
1956	596×2.4	802	628
1955	538×2.4	789	502
1954	452×2.4	811	274
1953	638×2.4	964	675
1952	768×2.4	920	923
1951	527×2.4	766	499
1950	497×2.4	974	219
1949	643×2.4	981	562
1948	662×2.4	941	648
1947	519×2.4	836	410

Appendix C

To acquaint the reader with a structured approach to form a promotional campaign, the following outline is suggested in Engel, Wales, and Warshaw, *Promotional Strategy* (Homewood, Illinois: Richard D. Irwin, Inc., 1967, pp. 515–18). The first part of this list is shown, since it is more concerned with the role of specialty advertising and what might be considered as preparation material for any campaign. The full outline also mentions selection of specific media, preparation of time and cost schedules, and actual preparation of advertisements.

AN OUTLINE FOR PLANNING A PROMOTION CAMPAIGN

Part I. Foundation Material for the Campaign

A. History and present status of firm and product
1. Date of establishment of company, including main periods of development, growth, decline.
2. Scope of present business, including number of products in the line; number and location of plants and selling offices.
3. Analysis of sales record during previous *five* years of particular product you have selected, focusing on reasons for any trends which are evident.
4. Financial condition of the company during previous five years with emphasis on its ability to conduct an adequate campaign. You should give company's past profit and loss figures, if available, as well as a ratio analysis.
5. Marketing policies, strategy, and organization of the company. What role does advertising play in relation to other forms of marketing effort?

6. Apparent profit inhibitors which may influence the campaign.
7. Brief analysis of previous advertising, concentrating on purposes of advertisements, appeals used, and an evaluation of general makeup of the advertisements. At least five examples of previous advertisements (including summaries of radio or television spots) should be placed in Appendix 1.

B. Diagram and brief description of distributive outlets used by your company in the sale of its product. The diagram should also show the normal channel or channels of distribution your product takes until purchased by consumer-buyers. In this discussion you should indicate the nature of the company's relationship with its dealers and the role they will play in the campaign.

C. The legal framework
   1. Discuss any legislation unique to your product which may affect the campaign.

D. The product
   1. Brief description of its important characteristics, with emphasis on major selling points.
   2. Ability of product to satisfy particular needs and wants of consumers.
   3. Possible changes that might be made to increase the utility of the product.
   4. Uses to which product may be put and the conditions under which it will be used.
   5. Seasonal fluctuations in the sale of the product.
   6. Indicate any factors that prevent or restrict the market for this product, such as customs, unfavorable climatic conditions, previous experience of consumers in certain areas, and other similar situations.

E. The market
   1. Market profile
      a) Type of people to whom your article is now sold. Show whether it is an article of general appeal or confined to certain income, racial, or other specific market groups.
      b) Indicate whether the market is national, sectional, or local, and any other geographic limitations.
      c) Indicate additional consumer groups that might be served and the possibility of appealing to them in this campaign.
      d) Develop a basis for determining the relative sales fertility or potentiality of each divisional market area.
   2. Qualitative aspects

    a) What is the motivation of potential buyers and users of both the generic product and the brand?

    b) Give the extent of use or ownership of the product and the market share of your brand if this information is available.

    c) How familiar are consumers and users with the brand? How frequently is it purchased?

    d) What is the image of the brand in consumers' eyes?

F. Present a list of the chief competitors of your product and five or more recent representative advertisements for each of these products (place in Appendix 2). Briefly analyze these advertisements, placing your emphasis on the distinction between these advertisements and those which were issued by your company during the same period.

G. Ultimate and immediate objectives of the campaign

  1. Discuss the mission of your company and its overall marketing goals (if known).

  2. State clearly and precisely the objectives which your advertising is expected to accomplish and the particular section or sections of the market you expect to cover. This section is the key part of your report, and it should receive considerable critical emphasis.

    Part II. The Financial Appropriation and Media Allocation

This section of the report is to include the following insofar as they are available:

A. The appropriation

  1. Brief analysis of *past* demand stimulation expenditures of the company, including:

    a) Total amount spent during the past year and over a period of five years to show the trend in such expenditures.

    b) The method used to determine these expenditures if such facts can be obtained.

    c) The apportionment of this expenditure to media and production costs if such information is available.

    d) All available data on the expenditures by the entire industry, groups of similar companies, and of individual competitors should also be included. In case no material is available for your company, the analysis must necessarily be based on the data for your industry.

  2. Analysis of the method or basis to be used in determining the size of the appropriation for *your* particular campaign.

    a) State briefly the particular method or methods which you are going to use.

    b) A statement of your reasons for using the particular method or methods. (Here you should consider: [1] company policy and previous experience with these methods; [2] the peculiar objectives of the campaign, state of product, specific purposes, etc.; [3] the financial situation of the company at the present time; and [4] market and competitive conditions affecting the advertising of your particular product.)

B. Brief summary of media used by company in previous campaigns. (This includes statements of both classes of media and also some of the better-known vehicles within a class, if known.)

C. Selection of major classes of media

  1. Which of the major classes of media are to be incorporated in the campaign? Be certain to state the reasons for using the media classes you have chosen, as well as the reasons for noninclusion of certain classes of media.

  2. What part of the total market do you expect to reach through each of these media?

  3. For what particular purposes is each medium best adapted? (Do you intend, for example, to utilize trade papers to secure dealer cooperation, class periodicals to carry your general sales message, and radio for purposes of good will advertising, or what?)

Index

This book has been set in 10 point and 11 point Times Roman, leaded 2 points. Chapter numbers are in 24 point Bodoni Bold #275 and titles are in 24 point Bodoni Medium #375. The size of the type page is 26 by 43⅔ picas.